AN ILLUSTRATED
HISTORY
OF
POLAND

Dariusz Banaszak • Tomasz Biber • Maciej Leszczyński
Translated with additional text by Richard Brzezinski

publicat
WYDAWNICTWO

Co-authors: Dariusz Banaszak, Tomasz Biber, Maciej Leszczyński
Translator and editor of the English edition: Richard Brzezinski
Editor of the Polish edition: Anna Sójka
Graphic design: Lech Siejkowski, Anna Cięciel-Łukaszewska, Elżbieta Kurczewska, Marian Winiecki
Computer/DTP support on the English edition: Zbigniew Wera
Technical editor: Roman Kalita

Cover illustrations:
Pope John Paul II, photo Indigo
"Portrait of Nicholas Copernicus", District Museum in Toruń, repr. Andrzej Skowroński
Royal Castle in Warsaw, photo Dariusz Krakowiak

Publicat S.A.
61-003 Poznań, ul. Chlebowa 24
tel. 061 652 92 52, fax 061 652 92 00
e-mail: publicat@publicat.pl
www.publicat.pl

OLD POLAND

POLAND PARTITIONED

POLAND REBORN

INTRODUCTION

An *Illustrated History of Poland* covers the story of Poland from the earliest settlements until the modern day. The book is intended for the young reader, but not only for the young – anyone interested in Poland will find here many interesting facts, anecdotes and pictures that illustrate the rich and eventful history of a nation now more than 1000 years old.

The book is divided into short, self-contained chapters, each telling the story of a particular king, dynasty, war or cultural theme. A chronology at the end of the book lists the most important events in a convenient form. Technical terms and Polish words which defy translation are marked by an asterisk (*); these are explained in a glossary on pages 124–125.

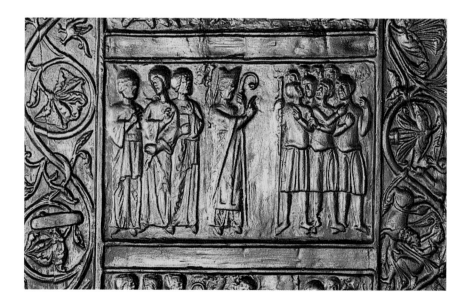

Centuries "Before Christ" (BC)

10th

9th

8th   738/737 BC – The Biskupin settlement is built

7th

6th

5th

4th

3rd

2nd

1st

1st   AD 1 – Traditional date of Christ's birth

2nd

3rd

4th

5th

6th

7th

8th

9th

10th   966 – Poland adopts Christianity

11th   1025 – Bolesław Chrobry is crowned

12th   1138 – Bolesław Krzywousty divides Poland

13th   1226 – The Teutonic Knights arrive in Poland

14th   1320 – Władysław Łokietek restores the monarchy

15th   1410 – Battle of Grunwald–Tannenberg

16th   1525 – The Prussian Homage

17th   1655–1657 – The Swedish "Deluge"

18th   1791 – Constitution of 3rd May

19th   1863 – The January Rising

20th   1939 – Hitler invades Poland

Centuries after Christ (AD)

A few notes on dates may help prevent confusion:

— A century is 100 years; a millennium is 1000 years.

— The modern calendar starts with the birth of Jesus Christ as year 1. Where confusion could arise, dates after Christ's birth are marked AD (*Anno Domini* – the Latin for 'Year of the Lord').

— Events that took place before the birth of Christ are dated with the abbreviation "BC" – Before Christ. (Note that years BC are counted in reverse – so that 738 BC is earlier than 400 BC).

— The year 966 is said to be "in the 10th century"; 1863 is "in the 19th century"; and 738 BC is "in the 8th century BC".

OLD POLAND

THE BISKUPIN SETTLEMENT

More than one thousand years before the Slavs arrived on the territory of modern Poland, a prehistoric people had set up a thriving culture. The fortress they built on an island at Biskupin is one of the best preserved Bronze Age settlements in northern Europe.

I n 1933 Polish archaeologists uncovered the remains of a Bronze Age fort at Biskupin in Wielkopolska*. Believed at first to be early evidence of Slavic settlement, the site became famous overnight. Biskupin is not the only prehistoric fortress settlement on modern Polish territory. Similar sites have been discovered in

THE SIMPLE LIFE

The wooden huts of Biskupin each had two or three rooms, and provided shelter for an average family of 10 to 12 persons. Each hut had a hole in the roof to let out the smoke from a stone fireplace.

AN ARCHAEOLOGIST'S PUZZLE

Until recently, most historians believed that the Biskupin settlement dated from 550 to 400 BC. After examining wood preserved in waterlogged soil, archaeologists in Poznań now believe the settlement

was in existence 200 years earlier. Tree-ring dating has shown that most of the oak was felled between 747 and 727 BC, more than half of it in the winter of 738/737 BC. The wood for the modern reconstruction (*above*) is some 2,700 years younger!

BISKUPIN ISLAND

The settlement as it would have appeared in the Bronze Age, with a wooden causeway providing the only access to the island. The lake has now largely silted up.

* Words marked by an asterisk are explained in the glossary on pages 124–125.

Silesia, western Pomerania and western Małopolska*. What is special about Biskupin is that the waterlogged soil of the area preserved the ancient wooden buildings to a high degree. Examining these structures revealed a great deal about the way of life of Poland's earliest settled inhabitants.

For its time, ancient Biskupin was certainly impressive. Wishing to protect themselves from enemy raids and wild animals, the early inhabitants chose to live on an island in the middle of a lake. The only way into the settlement was over a wooden causeway. A tall palisade set on a rampart made of wood and earth surrounded the site. The living quarters consisted of over 100 huts arranged in rows, divided by narrow streets. Because the site was boggy, these streets and all the walkways were covered with wooden boards.

The people of Biskupin spent most of their time farming, and were among the first in the Polish lands to use oxen for ploughing the land. They grew wheat, millet, barley and flax and, in separate gardens, poppy seeds, beans and peas. They harvested these crops with scythes made of bronze and, in later centuries, of iron. Archaeologists have unearthed the remains of blacksmiths' forges, and shoemakers' and potters' workshops – evidence that the Biskupinites were technically advanced.

Suddenly, at the beginning of the 5th century BC, probably after a rise in the water level of the lake surrounding Biskupin, the inhabitants abandoned the settlement. It was not until the 6th century AD – nearly 1,000 years later – that the site was again inhabited. Its new owners were the direct ancestors of modern Poles – a Slavic people known as the Polanians.

EVERYDAY LIFE IN BISKUPIN

The inhabitants of Biskupin had plenty to keep them busy. The women, besides looking after the children, prepared meals, made clothes from flax and wool, and pots from clay; and also tended the animals, which included cattle, pigs, sheep, goats, horses and dogs. The men built and maintained the ramparts, walkways and wooden huts. They helped with the farming, caught fish, gathered berries and hunted wild animals in nearby forests. It was also the duty of the men to keep a permanent guard on the ramparts. There was no school in Biskupin, but the children could not play all day. They helped with the daily chores, and by copying their parents, learned the skills they would need in adult life.

A.FONFARA.95

Baltic Sea

Biskupin

A KEY LOCATION

Biskupin is situated near Żnin in the modern province of Wielkopolska. The site was settled in the 8th century BC, because of its easily defensible location on an island. By the 8th century AD the Slavs had built a new wooden stronghold, as part of the Polanian princedom. In the early 11th century Biskupin became the property of the rapidly growing Church.

MIESZKO I

Many centuries after the inhabitants of Biskupin had abandoned their settlement and moved on, a new people arrived from the south-east – the Slavs. The first great ruler of the Polish branch of the Slavs was Duke Mieszko I.

By the 6th century AD, several Slavic peoples had arrived on the territory of modern-day Poland; among them were the Polanians, Vislani, Mazovians, Pomeranians, Lendizi and Slenzani. Their names survive today in geographical features, while the Lendizi are remembered in the Hungarian word *Lengyel*, meaning Pole. Other Slav peoples such as the Veleti and Sorbs had meanwhile penetrated as far west as the River Elbe in modern Germany. Over the next few centuries their settlements developed into organized states.

Each Slav state was based around a system of strongholds (*grody*)*. The more powerful the tribe, the more strongholds it controlled. At the head of each state was a duke, with his personal retinue of mounted soldiers and a council of tribal elders. The first duke to leave a solid footprint in the historical records was a certain Mieszko who lived from about AD 930 to 992. Mieszko ruled a large group of Slavic tribes known as the Polanians, so called after the open meadows (*pola*) in which they lived. At first, his lands extended over modern Wielkopolska and Kujawy, with their capital at Gniezno.

Mieszko had great ambitions, and wished to unite the neighbouring tribes under his control. Two major obstacles to his plans were a fierce Western Slav tribal group, the Veleti (also known as the Wilzi or "wolf people") who were raiding Mieszko's lands for plunder, and the Saxon border barons, who were pushing eastwards in search of new lands to conquer and settle, and who regarded Mieszko's people as pagan savages.

MIESZKO'S ANCESTORS

Siemowit – died *c*.900

Lestek (Leszek) – died *c*.930

Siemomysł – died *c*.960

The 12th-century chronicler Gallus Anonimus lists the forefathers of Mieszko I as Siemowit, Lestek and Siemomysł. This family later became known as the Piasts* after a legendary ancestor: a simple ploughman called Piast whose wife was named Rzepicha.

MIESZKO I
(c.930–992)

The first leader of the Poles recorded in historical documents was Mieszko I. Son of Siemomysł, he was probably born in Gniezno. He ruled the Polanians from 960 until his death in 992, and was buried in Poznań on the site of the modern cathedral.

DOBRAVA

The daughter of the Czech prince, Boleslav I Premyslid, Dobrava arrived in Gniezno in 965 to marry Mieszko I, sealing an alliance between the Polanians and the Czechs. Her wedding brought Roman Catholicism to the future peoples of Poland. Dobrava was the mother of Bolesław Chrobry. She died in 977.

The Slavic peoples of Mieszko's realm at the end of the 10th century. The Polanians later gave their name to Poland.

* Words marked by an asterisk are explained in the glossary on pages 124–125.

In view of these dangers, Mieszko made a treaty with the Prince of Bohemia, Boleslav I Premyslid, in which he agreed to abandon his pagan beliefs and to become a Christian. To seal the bargain he married Boleslav's daughter, Dobrava. She arrived at the Polanian court with priests who set about converting Mieszko and his subjects. The baptism ceremony took place in 966, a date which has been regarded ever since as the foundation year of the Polish state.

Mieszko's baptism brought his territories into the community of Christian countries. Now the Saxon barons had to treat him with the respect due to a Christian ruler. After defeating the Veleti in 967, and the Germans at Cedynia in 972, Mieszko was able to continue with the unification of the Slav tribes around him. The fruit of his labours was the country known in Latin – the language of the Medieval Church – as *Polonia*, from the name of Mieszko's tribe, the Polanians. This country we know today as Polska, or Poland.

THE BATTLE OF CEDYNIA

Mieszko fought many wars to acquire territory in western Pomerania and to defend his new lands from rival Slav tribes and German barons. In 972 at Cedynia (Zehde) near the River Oder south of Szczecin, Mieszko fought the Saxon margrave Hodo. After losing the first clashes, the Poles retired to the stronghold of Cedynia where, with the help of hidden reinforcements, Mieszko decisively defeated Hodo's knights. The battle, one of the first in Polish history for which the location is known, strengthened Mieszko's hold over western Pomerania.

The lands ruled by Mieszko I covered about 250,000 km^2, and were inhabited by about 1.2 million people.

Duke Mieszko I was baptised in the prince's chapel at Ostrów Lednicki. These pictures show the island and chapel ruins.

BOLESŁAW THE BRAVE

Mieszko's son Bolesław was even more ambitious than his father. He determined to create a pan-Slavic empire. Because of his great energy and military skills, he was later given the name Chrobry – "the Brave".

Taking over rule of the Polish lands after the death of his father Mieszko, Bolesław was faced by rival claims from his half-brothers and their mother – Mieszko's second wife, Oda. To secure his rule, he exiled them from Poland – this was typical of the decisive style that marked the rest of his reign.

In AD 997 the exiled bishop of Prague, Wojciech (Adalbert), organized a mission to convert the Old Prussians*, a pagan people who lived on the Baltic coast to the north-east of Poland. During the mission Wojciech was brutally murdered. His body was bought back by Bolesław for its weight in gold, and buried in Gniezno Cathedral; the Pope proclaimed him a holy martyr and saint. In a superstitious age, this was a highly important event – Poland now had a holy patron. The Pope took the opportunity to expand the Church's presence in Poland. An archbishop was installed in Gniezno, overseeing the work of three new bishops in Kraków, Kołobrzeg and Wrocław.

BOLESŁAW CHROBRY'S ARMY

Bolesław's wars against the Germans required a huge military effort. According to the chronicler Gallus Anonimus (who wrote 100 years later) Bolesław maintained a permanent force of 3,900 "armoured men" and 13,000 "shield-men". The typical armoured warrior (*shown at far right*) wore a mailcoat of linked iron rings, a metal helmet and a leather-covered wooden shield. He rode to battle on horseback and fought with a long spear and sword. The "shield-man" (*left*) was less well equipped; he carried a large almond-shaped shield, and a long spear was his main weapon. Only the wealthiest warriors owned swords, which were then very expensive items.

BOLESŁAW CHROBRY (967–1025)

The first crowned king of Poland succeeded his father Mieszko I in 992. His military successes won him the name Chrobry – the Brave. He was crowned King of Poland in 1025, but died in the same year.

SAINT WOJCIECH

Poland's first saint was killed during a mission to convert the pagan Old Prussians in AD 997. His martyrdom was depicted in the most important work of art of the early Piast period – the Gniezno cathedral doors, made probably by Flemish artists, *c*.1175. In the top scene Wojciech is seen baptizing the Old Prussians; in the lower scene he is murdered with an axe.

* No relation to the "German" Prussians, see the glossary on pages 124–125

BOLESŁAW CHROBRY'S EXPEDITION TO KIEV

In 1018, after winning the German war, Bolesław's armies marched south-eastwards to Kiev – the capital of the wealthy realm of Kievan Ruś. After a famous incident in which Bolesław chipped his sword on the gates of Kiev, his forces rode into the Ruthenian capital. Bolesław's main goal was to restore his son-in-law Swiatopelk to the Kievan throne. In this he was only partly successful, but the campaign marked the beginning of Poland's interest in the east, an involvement which would not always bring happy results. An oil painting of Bolesław Chrobry's celebrated entry into Kiev (*shown at left*) was made in the 19th century by Piotr Michałowski. Not knowing how Bolesław's warriors were dressed, the artist chose to show them as 17th-century Polish hussars, complete with wings! (*see page 51*).

It so happened that Bishop Wojciech had been a good friend of the German emperor, Otto III, who organized a pilgrimage to visit his tomb during the Church synod that met to inaugurate the new Polish bishops. In March 1000 – the dawn of the new millennium – Otto was welcomed to Gniezno by Bolesław the Brave in a magnificent ceremony. Greatly impressed, the Emperor placed his own crown on Bolesław's head, as a sign that he recognized the new Polish realm.

In 1002 Emperor Otto III died. His successor, Heinrich II, was far less friendly towards Bolesław and Poland. The Polish leader made things worse by attempting to acquire the lands of Western Slav peoples, whom the German emperor regarded as his subjects. A series of wars followed. Bolesław occupied Prague and the once-great Slavic realm of Moravia, holding it for several years. The treaty of Bautzen (Budziszyn) in 1018 put an end to the conflict by giving Bolesław control over two Western Slav tribal states – Lusatia and Milzenland (Milsko).

With peace in the west, Bolesław turned his gaze to the east, and launched an expedition into Kievan Ruś (Ruthenia), a wealthy territory equivalent to modern Ukraine. His troops reached Kiev with little difficulty. On his return journey, Bolesław added to his domains the so-called Czerwień Strongholds (*Grody Czerwieńskie*), which included Czerwień, Przemyśl and Sanok.

Nearing the end of his life, Bolesław crowned himself King of Poland. The ceremony took place on Easter Sunday 1025 in Gniezno cathedral. It was a event of international importance – a sign that Poland was now a first rate power in the Christian world.

THE SUCCESSORS OF BOLESŁAW THE BRAVE

Poland's first king, Bolesław Chrobry, had created a vast Slavic empire by conquest. His sons and grandsons proved unable to maintain the empire, and instead had to struggle to stop the Polish state from disintegrating altogether.

MIESZKO II LAMBERT (990–1034)

The eldest son of Bolesław Chrobry from his marriage with a western Slav princess, Emnilda, Mieszko II was also known by the Christian name Lambert. He was crowned king soon after the death of his father in 1025, but lost control of the realm in 1031 and fled abroad.

KAZIMIERZ ODNOWICIEL (1016–1058)

The son of Mieszko II and Rycheza, he ruled Poland from 1034, but was forced into exile by a revolt of the barons. He returned to Poland in 1039, and made great efforts to rebuild the war-ruined country. As a result he received the name Odnowiciel – "the Restorer".

After the death of Bolesław the Brave, the Polish crown was inherited by his son Mieszko II. The early years of Mieszko II's reign went well, but in 1031 he was faced by rebellion and war. The Hungarians abandoned an earlier Polish alliance, while the Germans and Ruthenians attacked Poland from both sides. The Western Slav regions of Lusatia and Milzenland (won by Bolesław Chrobry) were soon lost, and Mieszko II was forced to seek refuge in Bohemia. In Mieszko's absence his German wife, Rycheza, took the royal regalia to Germany. His brother Bezprym stepped in and attempted to tackle the crisis, but, soon fell victim to the chaos. Shortly before his death in 1034 Mieszko II was able to return from exile, but at the cost of recognizing the German emperor as his overlord. Mieszko's son Kazimierz succeed him, but because of the weakened condition of the Polish realm was never able to crown himself king.

Soon the chaos in Poland grew even worse. A violent pagan rising spread throughout the realm, destroying much of the hard work of the previous 70 years. The country broke up into regions, and Kazimierz was driven into exile. In 1038 the Czech prince Bretislav took the opportunity to invade. He seized Silesia, looted Kraków, Wrocław, Poznań and Gniezno, and took back to Bohemia everything of value he could seize, including large numbers of people. Gniezno with its cathedral was razed to the ground, as were many other towns. At the same time Poland lost control of the Czerwień Strongholds.

Returning to Poland in 1039, Prince Kazimierz began the enormous task of rebuilding his country. Gniezno, the ancient capital of the Polanians, was now a smouldering ruin, so Kazimierz shifted his base to Kraków (which became Poland's capital until 1596). Next, with help from the Germans and Hungarians, he recaptured Małopolska and Wielkopolska, and then, thanks to Prince Yaroslav of Kiev, he re-acquired Mazovia. His final prize was the retaking of Silesia from the Czechs in 1041. Kazimierz' successes in reuniting the realm earned him the name Odnowiciel – "the Restorer".

CANINE PUNISHMENT

An unusual penalty was meted out by Bolesław Śmiały to the wives of his soldiers who had cheated on their husbands while they were away on campaign. He ordered the unfaithful wives to breastfeed young puppies, while children born of their illegitimate liaisons were to be fed by bitches. This picture by an unknown artist, shows the king's bizarre punishment being carried out.

After Kazimierz's death in 1058 his eldest son Bolesław, known as Śmiały ("the Bold"), succeeded him. He followed in the footsteps of his great-grandfather, Bolesław Chrobry by sending an expedition to Kiev to assist Prince Iziaslav in regaining his throne. He also supported the Hungarian prince Ladislas I (who had been raised in Poland) and helped him obtain the Hungarian throne. But Bolesław's greatest feat was the freeing of Poland from dependence on the German emperor. He achieved this by taking advantage of a conflict between Emperor Heinrich IV and Pope Gregory VII over control of the Christian world. By supporting the Pope, who eventually won the contest, Bolesław Śmiały was rewarded with the title of King of Poland, and was crowned at Christmas 1076.

Bolesław Śmiały had successfully restored the status of Poland, but at great financial cost. When he devalued the nation's coinage to pay for this, he created enemies: one of them was Stanisław, Bishop of Kraków. The king ordered his execution in 1079. The brutal way in which the sentence was carried out caused a revolt of the nobles, and Bolesław was forced to flee to Hungary, where he soon died. His brother Władysław Herman took over the throne, but proved unable to maintain authority. He renounced his claim to the royal crown, and again acknowledged the German emperor as his overlord.

BOLESŁAW ŚMIAŁY (1040–1081)

Bolesław called Śmiały – "the Bold" – was the first son of Kazimierz Odnowiciel and Dobroniega. His policies were anti-German, though he took no direct military action against the Germans. Taking advantage of a conflict between the German Emperor and the Pope he crowned himself king of Poland in 1076, at the newly rebuilt cathedral in Gniezno. Exiled in 1079 as the result of a revolt of the nobles, he died in Hungary.

WŁADYSŁAW HERMAN (1042–1102)

The younger son of Kazimierz Odnowiciel and Dobroniega, he was also known by his German first name, Herman, as well as his Slavic name Władysław. His father probably gave him Mazovia to rule as an independent domain. After the exile of his brother Bolesław he was offered rule of the whole country by the rebel barons, but failed to rebuild the royal authority. He died in 1102 after dividing Poland between his sons, Zbigniew and Bolesław.

THE KILLING OF BISHOP STANISŁAW

Bishop Stanisław of Kraków (1030–1079) was the leader of a conspiracy of noblemen against King Bolesław Śmiały. In 1079 the king ordered him executed for treason by having his limbs chopped from his body. The gruesome sentence was carried out in the church on the Skałka Hill in Kraków – as shown in Jan Matejko's painting. Because it took place on holy ground, his death was seen as a martyrdom.
In 1253 he was canonized, and as St Stanisław became Poland's second patron saint – next only to St Wojciech.

BOLESŁAW WRYMOUTH

Known as Krzywousty ("Wrymouth") because of his crooked jaw, Boleslaw's reign was marked by a contest for power with his brother Zbigniew. Jealousy quickly led to war, and Poland as a whole was to suffer the consequences.

Władysław Herman died in 1102 leaving two sons, Zbigniew and Bolesław called Krzywousty ("Wrymouth"). The two brothers were never on friendly terms as both wished to rule. Their dispute developed into civil war, which ended with victory for Bolesław who chased his older brother out of Poland. Humiliated, Zbigniew sought help at the court of the German emperor, Heinrich V. The emperor ordered Bolesław to give his brother half of the country, and demanded tribute as the overlord of Poland. The young Bolesław refused, provoking a new war with the Germans.

After crossing the River Oder by a secret ford, Heinrich V's army attacked the Polish fortress at Głogów. It gallantly held out against all odds and eventually the emperor abandoned the siege. In smaller actions and skirmishes – for example, at Psie Pole near Wrocław – the German knights were gradually worn down and forced to return home. Emperor Heinrich had come to Poland for tribute: but, in the ironic words of the chronicler Gallus Anonimus, he left "carrying the bodies of his own slain as his tribute".

After the war Bolesław Wrymouth allowed Zbigniew to return to Poland, but quarrels soon broke out again. In

1112 Bolesław had Zbigniew blinded and thrown into a dungeon: he died soon afterwards. Wrymouth spent the rest of his reign doing penance for his brother's murder.

After fifteen years of hard campaigns to reconquer Pomerania, Bolesław dreamed of crowning himself king, but this he never achieved. Shortly before his death in 1138, remembering the bitter struggles with his brother and hoping to prevent the same from happening between his own sons, he announced his last will and testament. In it he divided Poland among his sons. The eldest, known as the "Senior", was to rule over the others and to represent the country abroad. He was also to decide on questions of war and peace, as well as to rule

THE SIEGE OF GŁOGÓW

In 1109 a German force led by Emperor Heinrich V attacked the Polish fortress of Głogów. The first assaults were thrown back, but the defenders knew they could not hold out for long. Hoping to buy time for Bolesław Wrymouth to bring a relief force, the townsfolk agreed to a truce, and handed over hostages. When the German emperor discovered that the Poles had no intention of surrendering he ordered the hostages hung from his siege towers, and launched an attack on the town

walls, imagining the Poles would not fire at the siege towers. He was wrong. In fierce fighting, the German assaults were pushed back. Precious days had been won by sacrificing the hostages, and when Bolesław's forces arrived the German emperor was forced to abandon the siege.

POLAND'S FIRST CHRONICLER

A Benedictine monk known as Gallus Anonimus – "the unknown Gaul" – wrote the first history of Poland. Working in Bolesław Krzywousty's chancellery between 1112 and 1118, he gathered information on the early Piast rulers. He was probably French, since "Gaul" was the old name for France.

BOLESŁAW KRZYWOUSTY (1086–1138)

He was called Krzywousty (Wry- or Crooked-mouth) because of a facial deformity: the muscles on one side of his face were lopsided. Archaeologists have also discovered that he had dark hair and a rather flat face.

over troublesome Pomerania, and to control the "Senioral" territory, which included the capital, Kraków, and other important towns in central Poland. Bolesław's solution looked ideal but it soon proved to be unworkable.

POLES ON THE BALTIC

After 15 years of war on the Baltic shores, Bolesław Wrymouth conquered eastern Pomerania, and made western Pomerania tributary to Poland. From this period come the words of a song preserved in the chronicle of Gallus Anonimus:
"Our forefathers made do with salted and foul-smelling fish;

We prefer fresh ones, still splashing in the ocean! Our fathers thought it enough to storm a land fortress; But the sea storms have no dread for us, nor the deafening roar of the waves. Our fathers were content to hunt for deer; We hunt for hidden treasures and monsters in oceans deep."

POLAND DIVIDED, 1138

On his deathbed Bolesław Wrymouth divided Poland among his sons: Władysław II "the Exile", received Silesia as well as the "Senioral" territory, which included the Kraków and Lęczyca regions, as well as parts of Kujawy and Wielkopolska; Bolesław, known as "the Curly-haired", received Mazovia and Kujawy; Mieszko "the Old" was given Wielkopolska; Henryk received the Sandomierz region and so was called Sandomierski. Bolesław's last son, Kazimierz Sprawiedliwy ("the Just") received nothing, as he appears to have been born after his father's death.

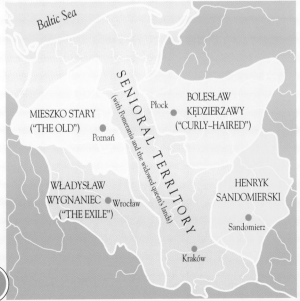

Baltic Sea

MIESZKO STARY ("THE OLD")
Poznań

SENIORAL TERRITORY (with Pomerania and the widowed queen's lands)

Płock

BOLESŁAW KĘDZIERZAWY ("CURLY-HAIRED")

WŁADYSŁAW WYGNANIEC ("THE EXILE")
Wrocław

HENRYK SANDOMIERSKI
Sandomierz

Kraków

POLAND DIVIDED

On his deathbed Bolesław Wrymouth shared out his lands among his sons, hoping to prevent discord between them. The result was the opposite of what he had hoped for – Poland disintegrated into rival dukedoms and was to remain divided for nearly two centuries.

Bolesław Wrymouth's son Władysław II, as the eldest son or "Senior", was authorized by his father's testament to supervise the entire territory of Poland. But he did not have much real power. When he attempted to subject his younger brothers to his plans they resisted, and so he attempted to remove them. Bolesław Kędzierzawy ("the Curly-haired"), Mieszko Stary ("the Old") and Wrymouth's last wife, Salomea – acting for the two minors, Henryk and Kazimierz – also wanted more power, and soon a civil war erupted. Before long Władysław II was defeated and fled to the German states. He accepted military support from the Germans, but this did not alter his plight. He was never able to return to power, and became known as Władysław Wygnaniec ("the Exile").

The idea of a "Senioral" territory, supervising the other Polish lands, had failed. Bolesław Wrymouth's divisions were sub-divided even further, as his sons, in turn, divided their lands among their own heirs. The fragmentation made Poland ever weaker. The situation was exploited by an aggressive western neighbour – the German March* (borderland) of Brandenburg. After conquering the lands of the Western Slav Veleti, the Brandenburgers seized the Lubusz area, and began to subdue the dukes of western Pomerania. A new and even darker era of conflict began in 1226, with the arrival to the north of Poland of another ambitious German power – the Teutonic Knights (*see panel at right*).

Despite the widespread destruction and misery in Poland during the period of fragmentation, there was progress in some quarters. Several princes were determined to see their lands prosper. Such was the case in Silesia, where Henryk Brodaty ("the Bearded"), grandson of Władysław the Exile, brought in settlers from Germany and the Netherlands, founded new towns, and encouraged crafts and trade. Henryk built up a powerful domain

RIDERS FROM HELL

The Mongols were fine horsemen, and could shoot bows even from horseback. Europeans had no idea where they came from and saw them as punishment from the Devil. They knew them as "Tartars" from the Latin word for the edge of the world – *Tartarus*.

WŁADYSŁAW WYGNANIEC (1105–1159)

BOLESŁAW KĘDZIERZAWY (1125–1173)

MIESZKO STARY (1126–1202)

* Words marked by an asterisk are explained in the glossary on pages 124–125.

with its capital in Wrocław, which included Silesia, Wielkopolska and Małopolska. The sudden arrival of the Mongols and the destruction they caused, brought the thriving realm of the Wrocław princes to a violent end (*see panels below*). The next leader to attempt to reunify the Polish lands was Henryk Brodaty's grandson, Henryk Probus ("the Just"). In his short reign he failed to convince the Pope to grant him the Polish royal crown.

Another Piast ruler with great ambitions was Przemysł II. After taking control of Wielkopolska and eastern Pomerania, he crowned himself king at Gniezno in 1295. Within a few months of taking the throne he fell victim to cut-throats hired by the Brandenburgers. It was to be several decades more before the Polish lands would again be united.

THE TEUTONIC KNIGHTS

The Teutonic Order, or to give its official name, the "German Order of the Hospital of the Virgin Mary in Jerusalem", was founded in 1190 during the Crusades. The knights of the order were known in Poland as *Krzyżacy* – from "Krzyż", meaning cross – after the black cross on their white garments.

The Order had been set up to defend pilgrims in the Holy Land. More aggressive ambitions developed when the crusaders were invited to Poland in 1226 by Konrad of Mazovia, grandson of Bolesław Wrymouth. Their task was to defend Mazovia against raids from a pagan Baltic tribe, the Old Prussians*. After defeating them, the German

Knights set up their own state, which they named after the pagan people they had all but annihilated – Prussia.

DEFEAT AT LEGNICA

The battle of Legnica (1241) against the Mongols ended in the complete defeat of the army of Prince Henryk Pobożny of Silesia, who was killed. The Mongols cut off his head and paraded it on a spear – as seen

in this painting. The Mongols, not wishing to waste time besieging the forts of Silesia, marched on into Hungary, but then, on hearing of the death of their Great Khan, returned home to Central Asia – to the great relief of all Europe.

HENRYK BRODATY
(c.1165/70–1238)

Henryk Brodaty ("the Bearded") was the son of the Silesian prince, Bolesław the Tall. He married a German princess Jadwiga (Hedwig), who later became a saint. In 1201 he succeeded to the Silesian throne, and was responsible for rapid economic growth.

PRZEMYSŁ II
(1257–1296)

Son of Prince Przemysł I of Poznań and Elizabeth, daughter of Henryk Pobożny. According to one medieval legend, he had his first wife Ludgarda killed because she was unable to provide him with children – it was rumoured that he had a servant suffocate her with a cushion.

THE REUNIFICATION OF POLAND

Broken into rival dukedoms for 200 years, it was not until the early 14th century that Poland was at last blessed with a monarch who, though short in height, had the stature to rebuild the country – Władysław Łokietek.

WŁADYSŁAW ŁOKIETEK (1260–1333)
He was crowned king of a reunited Poland in 1320, after receiving the Pope's approval. From that year Poland became a permanent kingdom.

WACŁAW II (1271–1305)
A member of the Czech Premyslid dynasty, he was already king of Bohemia (as Vaclav II or Venceslaus II), when he seized most of Poland.

After the death of Przemysł II in 1296, his lands were inherited by Władysław, the grandson of Konrad of Mazovia. Because of his small stature Władysław was called Łokietek, "the Elbow-High" – from a unit of measure of the time, the *łokieć* (ell), or elbow's length. For four years Łokietek ruled Wielkopolska and Pomerania, but he had enemies abroad and at home. After a dispute with Bishop Andrzej of Poznań he was excommunicated* and was forced, for many years, to seek refuge abroad.

In 1300 the Czechs of Bohemia, under Vaclav II of the Premyslid dynasty, seized Wielkopolska. Vaclav had already ruled Małopolska since 1291, and had forced a number of Silesian princes to swear allegiance to him. It was Vaclav who became the next monarch of Poland. The Czech king introduced a number of useful reforms, the most important being the creation of a new type of official known as a *starosta* or "elder", who ruled a small territory as the king's direct representative. But the Poles were never happy with Czech domination. After Vaclav II's death in Prague in 1305, his son Vaclav III succeeded him, only to be murdered in 1306. So ended the short period of Czech rule over Poland.

In the meantime, Władysław Łokietek had returned from exile. With the help of Hungarian troops he seized the duchy of Sandomierz, and after fierce battles occupied Małopolska. He placed garrisons in Kujawy as well as in eastern Pomerania and Gdańsk. His popularity rose, but not everything went well. In 1308 the Teutonic Knights seized Gdańsk by treachery, and within a year occupied the whole of eastern Pomerania. For the next 150 years Poland was to be denied access to the Baltic.

Łokietek had other problems in his capital, Kraków, where the German citizens revolted against his rule. (As in all Poland's cities at this date, the townsfolk of Kraków were a mixture of Germans and Polish-speakers.) Łokietek responded with force. He arrested the revolt's leaders, tied them to horses and dragged them through the

MASSACRE AT GDAŃSK

In 1308 an army of Brandenburgers laid siege to Gdańsk. The garrison of Gdańsk castle was too weak to defend itself, and Łokietek was busy elsewhere and unable to send help. The burghers of Gdańsk called on the Teutonic Knights for military aid, and offered to pay their costs. The arrival of the knights led the Brandenburgers to beat a hasty retreat. But the fighting was not over. In an act of supreme treachery, the Teutonic Knights attacked the town they had come to save. The houses of the townsfolk, both Polish and German, were burnt, and many people were slaughtered without mercy including women and children who had sought sanctuary in churches. The Knights then seized the rest of east Pomerania and the mouth of the Vistula.

* Words marked by an asterisk are explained in the glossary on pages 124–125.

ity streets. With the revolt crushed, Łokietek was free to conquer Wielkopolska, which he achieved in 1314.

After twenty years of hard work, on 20 January 1320, Łokietek achieved his great ambition, and was crowned king of Poland. The crown denied to Polish rulers for the entire 13th century was again on the head of a Piast. Łokietek's remaining years were spent trying to limit the expansion of the Teutonic Knights and to regain Pomerania. He took his legal case against the Teutonic Order to the Papal court, and won. But the German Knights ignored the verdict and stubbornly refused to hand over Pomerania.

In 1331 two armies – one Czech, the other of Teutonic Knights – marched deep into Poland, intending to combine forces. When the Czechs were delayed, Łokietek ambushed the retreating Teutonic forces at Płowce. Despite this victory Łokietek was unable, in the longer term, to prevent the Teutonic Order from annexing the territory of Kujawy. Late in 1332 the venerable old monarch became fell seriously ill. He died on 2 March 1333.

CORONATION SITE

Władysław Łokietek was crowned on 12 January 1320, along with his wife Jadwiga, at the royal cathedral on Wawel Hill in Kraków. The hill was the legendary home of King Krak, who had killed the dragon of the Vistula.

SZCZERBIEC, THE NOTCHED SWORD

The Polish coronation sword was first used by Łokietek. It was called *Szczerbiec*, after a sword notched by Bolesław Chrobry at Kiev in 1018.

THE BATTLE OF PŁOWCE

On 27 September 1331 at Płowce, Władysław Łokietek fought Poland's first major battle with the Teutonic Knights. Łokietek's forces were outnumbered, but he managed to ambush the German warrior-monks. Many prisoners were taken along with much of the German baggage. Although the battle was indecisive, it was a moral victory, and proved for the first time that the German knights, despite their heavy armour and superior resources, could be defeated.

KAZIMIERZ THE GREAT

It is often said that King Kazimierz III inherited a country of wood, and left one of stone. In this there is much truth, for as well as turning Poland into a major European power, he built over fifty stone castles.

When Władysław Łokietek handed over rule to his 23-year old son Kazimierz, he told him to rule justly and to regain the territories that had once been Polish. These were difficult tasks, but his son, who was crowned Kazimierz III, rose to the challenge.

Poland was still weak after decades of war. Peace was needed to allow the old power structures to be rebuilt. Kazimierz decided that the best solution was to end his quarrels by negotiation, even if this cost him dear. In 1335, at Vyshegrad in Hungary, he concluded a treaty with Bohemia. For the huge sum of 1,200,000 Prague *groschen**, the king of Bohemia agreed to abandon his claims to the Polish throne.

The Teutonic Order continued to be a problem. Like his father, Kazimierz III attempted to regain Pomerania from the German Order by legal means. He won the case, and the Knights were ordered on pain of excommunication to return all lands taken from Poland. Again, the verdict was never honoured. In the end, the two sides signed an "eternal" peace at Kalisz in 1343. Poland regained Dobrzyń and Kujawy, but at a high price: Chełmno and Pomerania including Gdańsk were acknowledged, for the first time, to be the property of the Teutonic Order.

Attempts by Kazimierz to increase his influence in Silesia led to a rekindling of war with the Czechs, and he was forced to abandon plans for southward expansion. Instead he turned east. In 1340 the Ruthenian prince Bolesław died. Assisted by Hungarian and Mazovian forces, Kazimierz seized Lwów and much of Red Ruthenia. The new eastern territory greatly increased the size of Poland and gave merchants a safer route to the Orient.

To improve the defences of his realm, Kazimierz set about a building programme the like of which Poland had never seen. Over fifty stone castles were erected and stone walls were built around thirty key cities. On the king's initiative many new towns and villages were established, fisheries were set up, and mills and granaries were built. The townsfolk and Jews were given privileges which greatly speeded the growth of trade and the crafts. The king reformed his treasury, and balanced his budget with the income from the salt mines near Kraków. He also reformed the legal system by standardizing the traditional laws of Wielkopolska and Małopolska; for the first time courts across the land passed similar sentences.

The year 1364 had special significance for the nation's capital, Kraków. In that year the king established

KAZIMIERZ THE GREAT (1310–1370)

An superb administrator, Kazimierz III was the only Polish monarch to earn the title "the Great".

THE RESTAURANT OF KINGS

During the famous 1364 Congress of Kings a rich councillor and merchant, Mikołaj Wierzynek, held a reception in his town house. The magnificence of the festivities has entered legend. Today a restaurant on the Kraków square is called Wierzynek.

Poland during the reign of Kazimierz Wielki.

MAĆKO BORKOWIC

In the third decade of his reign, a conflict erupted between Kazimierz III and the barons of Wielkopolska. Wishing to profit from new wars of expansion the rebels, led by the starosta of Poznań, Maćko Borkowic, announced that the King's peaceful policies were a sign of weakness. After several years of making trouble, Borkowic was captured and condemned to death by starvation in a dungeon.

THE PYRAMID OF POWER

Poland under Kazimierz the Great was a "layered" society. At its head was one man – the **King**. Lower down were four estates* or classes: the **Clergy**, the **Knights** (noblemen), and the **Burghers** (townfolk). The lowliest and most numerous estate were the Peasants or **Serfs**.

Poland's first university in the city. And when his daughter Elizabeth was married to the German emperor Karl IV, many illustrious visitors came to Kraków – among them the kings of Hungary, Denmark and Cyprus. It was a sign of Poland's increasing presence on the world stage.

When Kazimierz III died in 1370 he left a country that was more wealthy and secure than ever before, earning him the name "the Great". Although married four times, he died without a male heir, and was the last Polish ruler of the Piast dynasty.

FORTRESSES AND TOWNS

The most important settlements in early Piast Poland, were known as *grody** (strongholds or fortified-towns). Although built only of wood and earth, they made excellent centres for controlling the surrounding plains and were easily defendable refuges in time of war. As the stronghold grew in population, small sub-settlements with their own walls were added outside. In Bolesław Krzywousty's reign (1086–1138) Poland's fortress system numbered about 100 such fortified strongholds, each about 40 kilometres apart, and concentrated along frontiers and international routes.

From the 13th century, most new towns were established by charter according to German law. The site was selected by a local ruler, usually near an older settlement, and the town was laid out according to a set plan. Most towns were circular, and were surrounded by a stone wall, while streets were arranged a grid. Empty space at the centre was reserved for a square in which stood the town's administrative heart – the town hall.

CULTURE & TRADE UNDER THE PIASTS

The Piast period saw great changes in Poland. Over four centuries, the Piast rulers from Mieszko I to Kazimierz the Great transformed the country from a backward pagan dukedom into a civilized Christian monarchy.

When Mieszko I accepted Christianity in AD 966, he was allowing into Poland far more than just a new religion. Poland became part of the world of Latin Christendom, and Western culture came flooding in, transforming all aspects of life.

The presence of the Church in Poland was crucial in the modernization of the machinery of state. The clergy were rare in this brutal age in that they could read and write and had a smattering of knowledge about the world at large. They soon reached positions of trust, running the ruling lord's chancellery, and assisting in the day-to-day running of the realm. They also kept year-books or annals in which important events were recorded. It was from these that literature in Poland began, at first written in Latin. Soon Bible commentaries, lives of the saints, and even popular songs were being written down.

Another valuable service of the clergy was in education. This was greatly aided by the foundation of Poland's first monasteries in the 11th century, run at first by the Benedictines and later by the Cistercians. As well as being places for quiet contemplation, they were the schools and hospitals of their day.

Monasteries and churches were among the first stone buildings seen in Poland. Several were built in the first

SERVICE SETTLEMENTS

A special feature of early Piast Poland was the so-called service settlement. These small villages provided a lord and his officials with food, goods and services. Several such villages survive to this day, with names that give a clue to the occupation of their early inhabitants: Kołodzieje – where wheels

(koła) were made; Winogrady – whose inhabitants grew grape-vines, and Grotniki – where arrows and spears were fitted with metal heads (groty).

Silver penny (*denarius*) of Mieszko I – the first Polish coin.

The Latin name of Poland – *Polonia* – is first seen on silver pennies minted by Bolesław Chrobry.

Kazimierz the Great issued coins bearing the Piast eagle in an attempt to oust the popular Czech coinage from Poland. All in vain: after ten years his coins were no longer minted.

* Words marked by an asterisk are explained in the glossary on pages 124–125.

years of the 11th century, along with a few princely residences. They were decorated in the "romanesque" style fashionable throughout Europe. But it was not until brick appeared in Poland in the 13th century that the popularity of wooden buildings was challenged.

The Piast period saw a steady development of the economy. The livelihood of most Poles continued to be subsistence farming; but as agricultural methods improved – especially after the introduction of the three-field system in the early 13th century – food was grown in surplus, and could be traded for other goods. The production and trading of these goods was at first concentrated in small settlements nestled close to the walls of the main fortress (*gród*); these settlements expanded rapidly, and soon began to be replaced by a scatter of new towns.

Many new towns and villages were founded in the 13th century, especially in Silesia. Most were laid out and governed according to German law, giving them quite a different atmosphere from the traditional *gród*. The towns had a great deal of autonomy, which allowed citizens to live according to a different set of rules and customs than the country folk. Thousands of German, Flemish and Jewish settlers were attracted to Poland's towns by such freedoms; and the Jews were

even granted a royal charter in 1264, permitting them further privileges. This, of course, brought even more growth in crafts and trade.

Arab coins had been circulating in Poland long before the arrival of Christianity. At the end of the 10th century the first Polish coins appeared, but were valued more for their visual beauty than as money. Eventually the Piast rulers managed to convince their subjects that paying with coins was more convenient than the bartering of one type of goods for another.

Economic development brought with it social changes. In earlier centuries most of the population had been free peasants who worked their own land, providing occasional goods and services directly to the ruling prince. Now a large portion of the peasantry began to owe rents and services to powerful lords and churchmen. The peasant class became ever more distant from the ruling class, and a new middle estate* of rich and powerful men began to emerge. These noblemen – the *szlachta** – were to dominate the next period of Polish history.

ROMANESQUE STYLE

A new architectural style – romanesque – became popular throughout Europe between the 10th and 12th centuries. In Poland romanesque buildings were made of stone, since brick was not yet popular. Walls were thick, and windows small and narrow, with rounded arches. The ceiling vaulting was also rounded in shape and typically massive in structure. The picture (*right*) shows the 12th-century church of St. Prokop at Strzelno. At left is a romanesque column also from Strzelno.

MEDIEVAL CHRONICLES

The typical chronicle contained a list of historical events arranged by year, such as the births and deaths of princes, enemy attacks, and the appearance of comets. They were written by monks who worked in a special writing room or *scriptorium*. The picture shows a page of the famous Polish chronicle written by Gallus Anonimus.

THE FIRST POLISH UNIVERSITY

In 1364 Kazimierz the Great founded Poland's first higher seat of learning, the Kraków Academy. Later renamed the Jagiellonian University, it was one of central Europe's earliest universities, second to Prague. Courses were taught in law, medicine, mathematics and astronomy – all in the Latin language. The photo shows the courtyard of the university's oldest surviving section, the Collegium Maius.

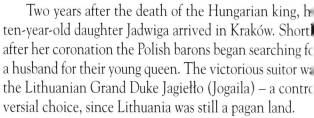

WŁADYSŁAW JAGIEŁŁO

With the death of the last Piast king, Poland's throne was inherited by the Hungarian branch of the Anjou dynasty, and soon passed to a ten-year-old queen, Jadwiga. Political necessity led to her marriage to a pagan man three times her age, the Lithuanian Grand Duke Władysław Jagiełło.

When Kazimierz the Great died without heirs the Polish throne passed to his nephew, the king of Hungary, Louis of Anjou, who became known in Poland as Ludwik Węgierski (Ludwik of Hungary). After his coronation in Kraków on 17 November 1370 he rarely visited Poland again, preferring to concern himself with his Hungarian kingdom. He left the rule of his Polish lands to various regents, the first of which was his Polish mother Elizabeth, who governed with the support of the Polish barons.

Like Kazimierz the Great before him, Ludwik was fated to have no sons. To secure the Polish throne for his daughter he was forced to grant privileges to the Polish nobles. In 1374 at Koszyce (now Kosice in Slovakia), Ludwik reduced the taxes on the noble class to a mere 2 *groszy* per *łan** (an area covering 40–60 acres worked by a single peasant family). It is from this statute that the Polish nobility began their rise to power, which was to have grave consequences for the future.

Two years after the death of the Hungarian king, his ten-year-old daughter Jadwiga arrived in Kraków. Shortly after her coronation the Polish barons began searching for a husband for their young queen. The victorious suitor was the Lithuanian Grand Duke Jagiełło (Jogaila) – a controversial choice, since Lithuania was still a pagan land.

The Lithuanians were a martial people related to the Old Prussians. From their marshy, forested Baltic homeland they had conquered vast territories extending as far as the Black Sea. The pagan Lithuanians had often raided into Poland, but at the close of the 14th century the powerful men of both countries agreed that they needed to forget their past differences and unite to face the common enemy – the Teutonic Order. In the summer of 1385, at Krewo in Lithuania, a "personal union" was concluded between Poland and Lithuania. Jagiełło would marry Jadwiga and be crowned King of Poland. The territories of Lithuania were to be combined with those of Poland, and Jagiełło was to strive to retrieve the lost lands of both states. The Grand Duke agreed to be converted along with his Lithuanian subjects. In February 1386 Jagiełło travelled to Kraków where he married the teenage Queen Jadwiga. On his baptism he took a new Christian name, Władysław, and so became known to posterity as Władysław Jagiełło.

A year later Jagiełło returned to Lithuania to complete the second part of his bargain: with the help of priests and monks, the conversion of the pagan Lithuanians began. But Jagiełło soon met with resistance. His cousin Witold (Vytautas) declared himself Grand

LUDWIK OF HUNGARY
(1326–1382)

Louis of Anjou was the son of the king of Hungary, Charles Robert of Anjou, and Władysław Łokietek's daughter Elizabeth. He was crowned King of Hungary (as Lajos I) in 1342, and as King of Poland (as Ludwik Węgierski) in 1370, but showed little interest in his Polish kingdom. He died in Hungary, leaving Poland to his daughter Jadwiga.

JADWIGA
(1373/74–1399)

Jadwiga (Hedwig) was the youngest daughter of Ludwik of Hungary. After marrying Jagiełło in her early teens, she devoted her life to helping the poor. She died in 1399 aged just 25, leaving all her valuables to fund the revival of the Kraków Academy which had declined after the death of Kazimierz the Great. It was later renamed the Jagiellonian University.

* Words marked by an asterisk are explained in the glossary on pages 124–125.

banner of Poland under Władysław Jagiełło

Duke and attempted to maintain Lithuania's separateness, even asking the Teutonic Knights for help. The conflict continued until 1401 when Witold acknowledged Jagiełło as the overall ruler, in return for which he received the title of Grand Duke for life.

The Polish–Lithuanian union and Lithuania's conversion to Christianity had unsettled the Teutonic Order. The German Knights no longer had the old excuse of a crusade against pagans when they wished to invade Lithuania. Another source of conflict was Poland's desire for access to the Baltic Sea – necessary if foreign trade was to develop. In the end, the direct cause of the new war was the seizure by the Teutonic Knights

POLAND AND LITHUANIA IN THE TIME OF JAGIEŁŁO

After the Treaty of Krewo (1385) Jagiełło's domain consisted of the Kingdom of Poland (often called the *Korona* – Crown), and the Grand Duchy of Lithuania. Despite having the same ruler, the two states retained separate identities. A further union in 1413 at Horodło brought Poland and Lithuania closer together by admitting Lithuanian boyars (noblemen) into the Polish knightly clans. The Horodło treaty also allowed the holding of joint meetings of the Seym*, and introduced in Lithuania (on the Polish pattern) the offices of *wojewoda** and castellan.

WŁADYSŁAW JAGIEŁŁO (c.1350–1434)

From 1377 Jogaila (called, in Polish, Jagiełło) ruled Lithuania. At the time of his invitation to take the Polish throne many in Poland believed him to be little more than a barbarian savage. The chronicler Jan Długosz, however, described him thus: "In height he was average, his face oval and thin, narrowing slightly at the chin. His head was elongated and almost completely bald ... candid, straightforward, there was not a trace of deceitfulness in him."

The "Great War" of 1409–1411 began when the Teutonic Order seized Samogitia, which separated its Prussian and Livonian lands.

▨ Territory recovered by Poland and Lithuania
▧ Tributary territories

of Samogitia (Żmudź) – the northernmost part of the Lithuanian realm which had remained addicted to paganism. So began the so-called "Great War" of 1409–1411.

The Grand Master of the Teutonic Order, Ulrich von Jungingen, had superbly trained troops, and could call to his aid knights from all over Western Europe. Jagiełło had a more varied army made up of Poles, Lithuanians and Ruthenians, together with small contingents of Tatars, Moldavians, Samogitians and Czechs. To bring together such a diverse force required skill and careful planning.

Towards the end of June 1410, Jagiełło's Polish contingent crossed a pontoon bridge over the Vistula built secretly at Czerwińsk. Once in the Order's territory, these troops combined with the Lithuanian, Tatar and Ruthenian contingents under Witold. Fearful of being outflanked, the Prussian Knights decided to fight, and a decisive battle took place on 15 July, near the villages of Grunwald and Stębark (Tannenberg). The fighting lasted all day, and as the chronicler Jan Długosz records "the King of Poland, not without great difficulties, won over the Teutonic Knights a complete victory." Thousands of German knights and their allies were killed, and the Grand Master Ulrich von Jungingen was among the dead. The captured standards of the German Order were cast at Jagiełło's feet. The Teutonic state would never be able to fully rebuild its military power.

Yet Jagiełło was unable to exploit his victory: his forces reached as far as the Order's headquarters at Malbork, but proved unable to capture the vital fortress. Eventually peace was signed at Toruń. Lithuania recovered Samogitia, but Poland had to make do with Dobrzyń. It was to be some time yet before the proud Prussian Knights were humbled into submission.

swords, 15th century

THE BATTLE OF GRUNWALD–TANNENBERG

On the morning of 15 July 1410, the armies of King Władysław Jagiełło and the Teutonic Grand Master prepared for battle. The German Knights were arrayed on an open plain, while the Poles and their allies were mostly hidden in the shade of a wood. Waiting for more detachments to arrive, Jagiełło delayed battle by having Holy Mass held twice. Impatient, and with his knights baking in the July sun, the Grand Master sent heralds with two swords to Jagiełło. Jan Długosz recorded their words in his history of the war: "The Prussian Grand Master Ulrich sends you and your brother by way of these messengers, two swords... that you will no longer hide among the woods and groves ... nor postpone the battle for later. If you believe there is too little room to deploy your ranks, the Prussian Master Ulrich ... will fall back on the plain that he has occupied with his army, as far as you desire. But finally chose whatever field of valour you desire, and put off the battle no longer." Jagiełło calmly accepted the swords and Ulrich duly drew back his forces. A furious battle ensued, with no respite until seven in the evening, by which time Ulrich was dead along with the cream his army.

helmet and breastplate in Gothic style, 15th century

lucerne hammer, weapon of a 15th-century footsoldier

BANNERS OF THE TEUTONIC KNIGHTS

banner of the Grand Master

HEADQUARTERS OF THE TEUTONIC KNIGHTS

Once called the "biggest pile of bricks north of the Alps", the fortress of Malbork (Marienburg) was the heart of the Teutonic Order's state. Building work began in 1276 and the fortress eventually comprised three levels: the Upper, Middle and Lower Castles. From 1309 to the mid-15th century Malbork was the residence of the Grand Master of the Teutonic Order. Although badly damaged by the Red Army in World War II, the fortifications have now been reconstructed.

JAGIEŁŁO'S SONS

Władysław Jagiełło died on 1 June 1434, leaving two sons – Władysław, aged ten, and Kazimierz, who was seven. Each was to rule in his turn, and each was to have a significant influence on the future of Poland.

Jagiełło's two sons were the children of his fourth wife, Sophia of Holszany. The elder son Władysław took the throne as Władysław III, but was too young to rule himself, so affairs of state were looked after by the talented bishop of Kraków, Zbigniew Oleśnicki. On his sixteenth birthday,

King Władysław III of Poland was also offered the throne of Hungary: keen for adventure, the youthful monarch accepted.

In this period Hungary was threatened by the growing power of the Islamic Ottoman Turks. The pope's representative and the Hungarian barons soon persuaded their new king to launch a crusade against the Turks. In 1444 Władysław marched at the head of a Christian army into Ottoman territory, and near Varna on the Black Sea coast, he fought a decisive battle. The initial attacks of his forces were successful, but Władysław was tempted to make a rash assault on the Turkish centre: he was quickly surrounded and killed. The battle was lost and the crusade came to an abrupt and tragic end.

After the disaster at Varna Poland was left without a king. In 1447, after a three-year *interregnum**, Jagiełło's second son ascended the throne as Kazimierz Jagiellończyk ("the Jagiellonian"), inheriting, at the same time, the Grand Duchy of Lithuania. The first years of his

a janissary – one of the Turkish sultan's elite footsoldiers

VARNA REMEMBERED

At the battle of Varna the young King Władysław III was killed during a rash attack. His head was removed by a janissary and preserved in a pot of honey before being proudly exhibited by the Turks. Shortly after the battle the believed site of Władysław's death was marked by a column, but in 1935 a far larger monument was erected in memory of the young king.

WŁADYSŁAW WARNEŃCZYK (1424–1444)

reign were spent re-establishing the royal power, which had been undermined by the barons. To secure his position he was forced to confirm the recently-won privileges of the nobles and, like his father before him, he granted even more rights. One effect was the rise of noblemen's local assemblies – the so-called dietines (*seymiks**). These would soon influence the most important affairs of state.

Kazimierz Jagiellończyk's greatest success was the recovery of eastern Pomerania with Gdańsk from the Teutonic Order, as a result of the Thirteen Years' War of 1454–66. The conflict began when the Teutonic Order prevented its subjects from trading with Poland, and imposed penalties on merchants who disobeyed. In February 1454 a delegation from the Prussian towns came to Kraków. On King Kazimierz's promise that he would send military support, the key towns of Prussia (Gdańsk, Toruń and Elbing) formed the Prussian League and broke away from the Teutonic state. A new conflict began.

The war did not begin well. At the battle of

KAZIMIERZ JAGIELLOŃCZYK (1427–1492)

Grand Duke of Lithuania from 1440, and king of Poland from 1447; his wife Elizabeth of Habsburg, "the mother of kings", had six sons and seven daughters. Kazimierz's greatest achievement was victory in the Thirteen Years' War (1454–66) over the Teutonic Knights.

Chojnice in September 1454 the Poles were defeated. But an important lesson was learned – to win against the Teutonic Knights, it would be necessary to recruit an expensive army of professionals. The royal treasury was empty. So, reluctantly, Kazimierz was forced to grant new privileges to the nobles before they would approve more taxes. At Nieszawa (1454) he agreed not to call out the Feudal Levy* of nobles to war, nor raise new taxes, without the approval of the dietines. With the necessary funds raised, the war at last turned in Poland's favour.

Victory over the Teutonic Order in 1466 brought Poland greater status in Europe. The Jagiellonian dynasty also went from strength to strength. Besides Poland and Lithuania the Jagiellonians controlled much of central Europe – Władysław, the eldest son of Kazimierz Jagiellończyk ruled as king of Bohemia (1471–1516) and of Hungary (1490–1516).

THE PRUSSIAN TOWNS

In 1454 the wealthy towns of Prussia sought help from the Polish crown against oppression by the Teutonic Knights. After 13 years of war with the Teutonic Order a treaty was signed at Toruń (*above*).

Under its terms the Prussian towns were able to prosper from the grain trade along the River Vistula. The grain was loaded onto ships by wooden cranes, such as the famous Żuraw (Great Crane) in Gdańsk harbour (*below*).

PRUSSIA PARTITIONED

The defeat of the Teutonic Knights in 1466 saw their Prussian lands divided. The western half, "Royal Prussia", became a self-governing province of Poland, while

"East Prussia" remained under the Grand Master but became a Polish fiefdom.

▨ Territory handed to Poland after the war. Regions tributary to Poland after the war.

* Words marked by an asterisk are explained in the glossary on pages 124–125.

POLISH SOCIETY IN THE 15TH CENTURY

The end of the Middle Ages brought great social change in Poland as the warrior knights gave up warfare and became noble landowners. By turning their energies to farming, they transformed the Polish landscape and the Polish economy.

I n Poland, the knightly class had emerged as a distinct group during the reign of Kazimierz the Great (1333–70). Ideals of chivalry and the insignia of knighthood had been inspired by western European trends, and, in truth, Polish knights differed little from those in Germany. Poland, however, adopted its own unique system of heraldry – based on the *herb** or clan-badge – quite unlike that seen in the West.

When, in the 1450s, Poland went over to an army of professional soldiers, the reason for the existence of warrior knights began

JAN DŁUGOSZ (1415–1480)

The chronicler Jan Długosz (Longinus) was one of the greatest scholars of his age. His interest in history was inspired while studying liberal arts at the Kraków Academy. This passion developed further in the service of the bishop of Kraków,

Zbigniew Oleśnicki (1389––1455). Bishop Oleśnicki hired Długosz to immortalize himself and the battle of Grunwald in which he had personally saved the king from a German knight's lance. Magnificent coloured illustrations in Długosz's *Banderia Prutenorum* showed the banners won from the Teutonic Knights at Grunwald, which in Długosz's day hung in Kraków Cathedral. More ambitious still was Długosz's epic history of Poland, much of which concerned the "Great War" of 1409–11. Because of his wide-ranging knowledge, King Kazimierz Jagiellończyk appointed Długosz as tutor of the royal children.

KNIGHTHOOD

During the Middle Ages a warrior class, the knights, emerged as the elite of society, both in Western Europe and in Poland. Knights had their own elaborate etiquette and customs. A prospective knight first served at the court of a lord where, as a page, he learned the

manners of the court and the craft of war. Next he went on military service as a squire, the assistant to a knight. At about 20 the young man was made a knight by his lord or the king, by being "dubbed" three times on the shoulder with a sword. Only then was he permitted to wear the symbols of knighthood – an ornate sword belt and gilded spurs.

In peacetime, knights maintained their readiness for war by jousting in tournaments. These were fought according to strict rules – the object being to unhorse the opponent with a blunt lance. Although dangerous, great fortunes and royal favours could be won by the victor.

* Words marked by an asterisk are explained in the glossary on pages 124–125.

to disappear, and they were forced to seek less warlike occupations. Most found a new role in agriculture, and the "noble-knight" gave way to the "noble-landholder". Huge manorial farm-estates (*folwarki**) sprang up all over the fertile Polish meadowlands. The harvests, especially of grain, brought in large sums of money, and soon Poland's noblemen were growing fantastically rich.

The trading and shipment of this grain also brought wealth to Poland's cities, especially to the port of Gdańsk (Danzig). The burgher class expanded rapidly, and began to organise the first tradesmen's associations or guilds, which supervised the training of apprentices, and maintained quality standards. Guilds were created for everything from goldworking to baking and from painting to tailoring. The guilds were at the very heart of the growth and wealth of Poland's towns.

Much of the new money was invested in buildings, built in a new architectural style – gothic. It took its name from the pagan Goths who had destroyed the Roman empire – probably because the new style was such a contrast to the romanesque popular before it. New slender and elegant gothic churches brought a dignified appearance to Poland's flourishing towns.

The Kraków Academy also benefited from the new wealth, and grew rapidly in the late 15th century. Many foreigners – mainly Germans, Czechs and Hungarians – studied at the Academy. Lectures were given by Polish professors famous throughout Europe, such as Paweł Włodkowic and Wojciech of Brudzewa. Among the students was Jan Długosz, Poland's first true historian.

WIT STWOSZ'S ALTAR

The 15th century saw the blossoming of art in Poland's cities. Among the greatest works was the altarpiece of St. Mary's Church in Kraków. Made between 1477 and 1489 by the German sculptor Weit Stoss (known in Poland as Wit Stwosz), it is regarded as one of the finest examples of its type in Europe. Stoss's altarpiece took the form of a "triptych" – with three panels, the outer ones opening to reveal a magnificent central scene. The altar's human figures are arranged in scenes of the life of Jesus, and are sculpted in the realistic manner so typical of gothic art.

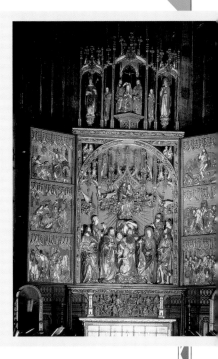

This half-*grosz** coin with the crowned eagle of Poland was minted at Kraków at a time when coinage was being widely faked. The chronicler Jan Długosz records that in 1467 Władysław of Domaborze, castellan of Nakło, was condemned to death for illegally minting coins in his castle.

GRAIN-BASKET OF EUROPE

The growth of Europe's towns in the 15th century led to a surge in the demand for farm produce, and agriculture suddenly became a profitable business. These changes occurred just as Polish noblemen-knights were seeking more peaceful occupations. They set up huge manorial estates – known as *folwarki* – which produced grain mainly for the international market. The nobleman used local peasants as his workforce. In exchange for the right to live on the nobleman's property, the peasants had to work the land for a specified number of days per week. In time these "labour dues" were increased, effectively turning the peasants into slaves. By the mid-16th century Poland was exporting hundreds of shiploads of grain via Gdańsk, and had become known as the "grain basket of Europe".

GOTHIC

A new style of architecture known as gothic reached Poland from Normandy and Burgundy in the 15th century. One of the best examples in Poland is Gdańsk Cathedral (*right*). Gothic churches had many slim towers, surmounted by pointed spires. Vast stained-glass windows brought a dazzling new light and atmosphere to church interiors.

THE LAST JAGIELLONIANS

The great Jagiellonian dynasty continued to rule Poland–Lithuania for the first three-quarters of the 16th century. The period was marked by the birth of the "noble democracy", and the final humbling of the Teutonic Knights.

After the death of Kazimierz Jagiellończyk, his son Jan Olbracht succeeded to the Polish throne. His reign was marked by the further weakening of royal authority, and an increase in the rights of the nobles. Eventually most of the state's power was in the hands of the Seym* or parliament, in which representatives of the regional dietines (*seymiks**) sat with the king and his advisors to debate the issues facing the country.

JAN OLBRACHT (1459–1501)

The third son of Kazimierz Jagiellończyk, Jan Olbracht (John Albert) is usually remembered for the disaster that befell the noblemen of the Feudal Levy* who were massacred during an expedition into the Bukovina forest in Moldavia in 1497. It was during his reign that the Seym shaped itself into the main institution of government of the Polish Commonwealth.

ALEKSANDER (1461–1506)

Kazimierz Jagiellończyk's fourth son was probably the least talented. From 1492 he ruled in Lithuania as Grand Duke, but attempted to run it independently of Poland. In 1495 he married the Muscovite tsar's daughter Helena. After taking the Polish throne in 1501 he proved unable to maintain order. His feeble rule led to a long-term decline in the power of Poland's kings.

In 1501 the throne passed to Jan Olbracht's brother, Aleksander. He was forced to sign the Mielnik Privilege of 1501, which effectively put rule into the hands of the Senate. The incompetent rule of the senators, who were mostly wealthy magnates, led the lesser noblemen to act. At the Seyms of Piotrków (1504) and Radom (1505) the Senate's powers were curtailed. The Radom Seym saw the passing of an important statute, known by its Latin name, *Nihil Novi* – "Nothing New". It forbade the king and Senate from making any important state decisions without the approval of the lesser nobles. "Nothing about us without us" (*Nic o nas bez nas*) became the slogan of noblemen's rights, and a new form of government, the "noble democracy", was born.

The next Jagiellonian on the Polish throne was Zygmunt (Sigismund) I. He attempted to carry out a prudent political programme with the support of the magnates, and was ably assisted in this by his Italian wife, Bona Sforza. Born into a powerful family herself, she was a champion of strong royal rule.

Zygmunt I's great achievement was the final ending of the problem of the Teutonic Order. The 1466 Treaty of Toruń had brought peace with the German knights, but in the first decades of the 16th century disputes erupted again. The Grand Master, Albrecht von Hohenzollern, was determined to make the Teutonic Knights independent of Poland. When he refused to pay homage to the Polish king he sparked off a new conflict. This, Poland's last war with the Teutonic Order, began in 1519, with Polish troops occupying large areas of the Prussian state and laying siege to the Order's capital at Königsberg. The conflict continued, with breaks, until 1525, when Martin Luther's reformation reached Prussia and the Grand Master took up the Lutheran creed. As a result the Teutonic Order closed down its operations in Prussia, and the monastic state became an ordinary dukedom. The Grand Master now became simply a duke, and was obliged to pay homage to Poland. One of Poland's greatest enemies had disappeared from the map. But the victory was a hollow one, for the new Prussian state was eventually to become a dangerous rival of Poland.

The 1550s and 1560s saw an epilogue to the story of the Teutonic Knights, with the collapse of the Order's

* Words marked by an asterisk are explained in the glossary on pages 124–125.

ZYGMUNT I STARY (1467–1548)

The fifth son of Kazimierz Jagiellończyk, in 1506 he became grand duke of Lithuania and king of Poland. Indecisive in politics, he was, however, highly religious, and managed to fight off the Lutheran reformation. His reign marks the beginning of the golden age of Polish culture.

THE PRUSSIAN HOMAGE

After defeat in the war of 1519–21, the Grand Master Albrecht von Hohenzollern closed down the Teutonic Order in Prussia. In 1525 he paid homage – as Duke of Prussia – to King Zygmunt, as depicted in Jan Matejko's famous painting.

footsoldier's sword, 16th century

Livonian* branch in Latvia and Estonia. A Livonian War broke out, with Poland–Lithuania, Sweden, Denmark and Muscovite Russia each fighting to keep or seize the strategically important Livonian ports. Poland temporarily obtained the larger part of Latvia, and more permanently gained Kurland and Semigalia as fiefs. But the cost was high – Poland was drawn into a bitter conflict for domination of the Baltic Sea, which was to last until the 18th century.

Zygmunt II August had succeeded his father as king of Poland in 1548. When it became certain that he would die without an heir, he decided to bring Poland and Lithuania closer together. In 1569 a Seym of Polish and Lithuanian deputies was called at Lublin. After a furious debate, differences were settled and an Act of Union was signed, the main points of which were as follows:

• Poland and Lithuania to be united as a "Commonwealth (*Rzeczpospolita*) of Two Nations".

• The Commonwealth to be ruled by an elected king, and by a Seym with deputies from both countries.

THE UNION OF LUBLIN

The 1569 Act of Union signed at Lublin (*photo above*) brought the population of the Polish–Lithuanian Commonwealth to 8 million, with Poles numbering about 40 percent (3 million) of the total. Overnight Polish society became multi-cultural, with large minorities of Ruthenians (Ukrainians and Byelorussians), Jews, Germans, Armenians and Tatars.

"The Union of Lublin" as visualized by Jan Matejko

- Lithuania to keep its own laws, institutions, treasury and army.
- The provinces of Podlasie and Volhynia, plus the Ukraine to be transferred from Lithuania to Poland.

Three years later Zygmunt II, the last male of the Jagiellonian dynasty to sit on the Polish throne, died.

ZYGMUNT II AUGUST (1520–1572)

The son of Zygmunt I and Bona Sforza. Unusually, Zygmunt (Sigismund) II was crowned king in 1529 during his father's lifetime, and ruled in Lithuania from 1544. His efforts to unite the two states resulted in the Union of Lublin (1569). Although married three times, he died childless.

THE SEYM

Poland's diet or parliament, the Seym was the state's highest legislative body and reached its final form in the 16th century. It met every two years for a six-week session, though in emergencies "extraordinary" seyms would sit for up to two weeks. Sessions were held in different towns: Kraków, Warsaw, Grodno, Piotrków Trybunalski and Lublin. The Seym had two houses, the Senate and the Chamber of Deputies, with the King leading the Senate, and an elected Marshal presiding over the Deputies. At the beginning and end of each session both houses sat together, but otherwise debated separately. The business of the Seym included passing laws, balancing the budget, raising taxes, and paying the army. It could also discuss foreign alliances and declare war on foreign powers.

THE KING

SENATORS
(Bishops, *wojewodas*, office-holders of Poland and Lithuania)

DEPUTIES
(Provincial representatives, chosen at local dietines)

RULERS OF POLAND

PIAST DYNASTY

MIESZKO I
(c.960–992)

BOLESŁAW CHROBRY
(992–1025)

MIESZKO II LAMBERT
(1025–1034)

KAZIMIERZ ODNOWICIEL
(1034–1058)

BOLESŁAW ŚMIAŁY
(1058–1079)

WŁADYSŁAW HERMAN
(1079–1102)

BOLESŁAW KRZYWOUSTY
(1107–1138)

THE PERIOD OF FRAGMENTATION

WŁADYSŁAW ŁOKIETEK
(1306–1333)

KAZIMIERZ THE GREAT
(1333–1370)

ANJOU DYNASTY

LUDWIK OF HUNGARY
(1370–1382)

JADWIGA
(1384–1399)

JAGIELLONIAN DYNASTY

WŁADYSŁAW JAGIEŁŁO
(1386–1434)

WŁADYSŁAW OF VARNA
(1434–1444)

KAZIMIERZ JAGIELLOŃCZYK
(1447–1492)

JAN OLBRACHT
(1492–1501)

ALEKSANDER JAGIELLOŃCZYK
(1501–1506)

ZYGMUNT I STARY
(1506–1548)

ZYGMUNT II AUGUST
(1548–1572)

POLAND'S GOLDEN AGE

The 16th century saw art, architecture and science flourish in Poland as never before. Six centuries after its foundation, the country suddenly became a powerful and cultured nation.

The blossoming of Polish culture began during the reigns of the last two Jagiellonian kings, Zygmunt I Stary (1506–1548) and Zygmunt II August (1548–1572). This transformation was greatly assisted by Poland's close connections with Italy – through Bona Sforza, Zygmunt I's Italian queen, and the many Poles travelling to study in Italian universities. Two new intellectual movements arrived from Italy. The first was the "Renaissance", meaning rebirth. It was the rapid development of art, science and literature, modelled on the ancient cultures of Greece and Rome. The second was "humanism" – a revived interest in human beings and everything connected with them. The changes were first visible at the royal court, with foreign noblemen, artists and scholars influencing the tastes of the immediate royal circle and the magnates. Soon the whole atmosphere of the age had changed. The medieval obsession with death was swept under the carpet, and the adage *memento mori* ("remember you will die") was forgotten. In place of it all came a new appreciation of beautiful objects and the love of pleasure for its own sake.

Another crucial innovation was the printing press. As well as being instrumental to the boom in science and learning, it was at the centre of the popularization of

THE "ZYGMUNT" BELL

Poland's most famous bell was hung in the tower of Wawel Cathedral in the reign of Zygmunt I. Massive in size and deafening in sound, it is rung only on important state occasions.

PIESKOWA SKAŁA

The reworking of Wawel Castle in Italian fashion inspired many magnates to rebuild their own houses in a similar style. The manor house of the Szafrański and Zebrzydowski families at Pieskowa Skała is a fine surviving example.

WAWEL CASTLE

The seat of Poland's kings was the castle on the Wawel Hill in Kraków. The main courtyard, with its splendid Italianate galleries opening into large and well-lit rooms, was substantially rebuilt between 1507 and 1536.

THE WAWEL TAPESTRIES

The royal chambers of Wawel castle are today adorned by a series of colourful wall tapestries known as "arrases" after the first place of manufacture of such fabrics – Arras in France. Zygmunt August collected nearly 350 arrases, most showing Biblical and hunting scenes.

Polish as a written language. Without the printed book, the discoveries of Copernicus would have taken longer to reach the world at large; just as importantly, the wit of Mikołaj Rej and the sublime poetry of Jan Kochanowski might never have been written down.

Printing also had a great impact on the reformation of the Church. As had happened first in Germany, the Polish clergy were criticized for their excessive lifestyles, and the need was voiced for a return to basic Christian values. Many Polish nobles, townsfolk and even peasants were persuaded to change their religion. The new Polish Protestants included Lutherans and Calvinists, as well as the fraternity known as the *Arians**, who put great weight on education and did not believe in shedding blood. In contrast to most other European countries, the followers of the various religious faiths were not persecuted. While heretics abroad were being burnt at the stake by the hundred, in Poland they were tolerated; indeed, Poland became known as the "land without stakes".

THE CULINARY QUEEN

Bona Sforza (1494–1557), the wife of Zygmunt I, came to Poland from Italy in 1518. She brought with her many foods which had never been seen in Polish kitchens. Several vegetables, including celery, leeks and lettuce were first eaten in Poland during Queen Bona's reign.

THE PEARL OF POLAND'S RENAISSANCE

The 16th century saw the growth and beautification of Poland's towns. One of the most impressive civic buildings of this period that survives today is the Poznań *ratusz* or town hall. It was designed by the Italian architect Giovanni Baptista Quadro.

MIKOŁAJ REJ (1505–1569)

Called the father of Polish literature, he was the first poet to write in Polish rather than Latin. A great observer of human weaknesses, his witty and often ribald verses and ditties made fun of people who took themselves too seriously.

JAN KOCHANOWSKI (1539–1584)

Poland's greatest Renaissance poet. He wrote song lyrics and amusing epigrams and, after the death of his daughter Urszulka, beautiful melancholy poems. He was also the author of Poland's first tragedy, *The Briefing of the Greek Deputies*.

NICHOLAS COPERNICUS (1473–1543)

His wide interests ranged from politics and economics to literature and medicine, but he became famous as an astronomer. In his book *On the Movements of Celestial Bodies*, he announced his discovery that the Earth moves round the Sun.

* Words marked by an asterisk are explained in the glossary on pages 124–125.

THE FIRST ELECTED KINGS

The death in 1572 of Zygmunt August, the last king of the Jagiellonian dynasty, left Poland in a crisis. The method for choosing a new ruler should the old monarch die without an heir had never before been established.

For some time it was debated how a new king should be selected. Finally, everyone agreed in principle that the whole nobility should be allowed to decide. They would gather for this purpose near Warsaw, and vote in a "Free Election". Meanwhile, in the uncertain interlude between the death of an old monarch and the election of a new one, the country would be ruled by an *interrex* or "between-king", namely the *Prymas** (Primate) of the Polish Church.

In 1573 four candidates stood in the first Polish free election: Henryk Walezy (Henri de Valois, brother of the King of France); the Russian tsar, Ivan IV "the Terrible"; Archduke Ernest of the Austrian Habsburg dynasty; and the King of Sweden, Johan III Vasa. The Polish nobles gathered *en masse* (and in some disorder) and made their choice – it was Henri de Valois.

THE ELECTION FIELD

From 1573 Polish kings were elected rather than born to the throne. The election was held in a large field at Wola near Warsaw. Every Polish nobleman was eligible to vote, and in practice up to 15,000 did. Mounted on horseback, they assembled behind the banners of their provinces. The result was determined when they shouted in unison the name of the new king. Arguments were common and often degenerated into mass scuffles leading to scenes of utter confusion.

Corruption was rife, with money changing hands to obtain support for a candidate. Another problem was the Warsaw location, which drew many poor nobles from nearby Mazovia, who were the easiest to bribe.

HENRYK WALEZY (1551–1589)

Henri de Valois was the son of King Henri II of France. He was Poland's first elected king, but ruled for only four months after his coronation in Kraków in February 1574.

His name was preserved in the Henrician Articles – conditions to which each elected king of Poland had to swear on his coronation. The Articles forbade the elected monarch from making state policy without the approval of the Seym. If the king broke the Articles or interfered with the nobles' privileges, they were in their rights to refuse to obey him. After returning to France Henri took the French throne as Henri III. He was soon drawn into the civil war between French Catholics and Huguenots, and was assassinated by a monk in 1589.

STEFAN BATORY (1533–1586)

Prince of Transylvania from 1571, and king of Poland from 1576. His firm-handed rule was not always popular with the nobility, and when he died in 1586 there were rumours of poisoning.

* Words marked by an asterisk are explained in the glossary on pages 124–125.

The young Henri looked like the perfect new king, but this was not to be. He had arrived in Poland in a cold January, when the country was at its bleakest and most unwelcoming. After ruling for just four months he received news of the death of his brother Charles IX of France, and escaped in the night, returning to take the French throne as Henri III. Poland was again without a king, and it was two years before a replacement could be agreed on. After another Free Election, a new monarch was duly chosen – the Transylvanian, Stefan Batory.

Batory at once made it clear that he would not be a "puppet" king. He went to work restoring order and imposing his own brand of rule on the Polish nobles. In 1577 he ruthlessly put down a revolt by the citizens of Gdańsk, who were attempting to cede from the Polish Commonwealth. His greatest achievement, however, was the winning of the Livonian War against Muscovite Russia.

To achieve this task he introduced wide-reaching reforms in the army, and then launched three epic campaigns deep into Muscovite territory. In 1579 his forces captured the fortress of Połock; in 1580 they took Wielkie Łuki; in 1581 they were about to take the huge stone-walled city of Pskov when the Russians sued for peace. At the treaty in 1582 the disputed territories in Livonia where handed to Poland in exchange for Batory's conquests.

With such victories behind him, Batory made plans for a great "crusade" against Turkey, but these dreams collapsed when he died suddenly in 1586.

Eastern-style *bekhter* armour. This example was made in Poznań in 1580, in imitation of suits worn in Muscovite Russia.

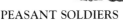

PEASANT SOLDIERS

King Stefan Batory made important reforms in the army, helping to bring it up to western standards. Poland had long suffered from a lack of foot soldiers, so he introduced – for the first time – recruitment among Polish peasants. They were known as *Wybraniecka* infantry, because one man was to be "selected" (in Polish, *wybrany*) from every 20 farms on royal land. As a result, the Polish army received its first 2,000–3,000 peasant soldiers, who played an important part in the sieges of the Livonian War.

JAN ZAMOYSKI (1542–1605)

Chancellor of Poland and *Grand Hetman** of the army, Zamoyski was the constant aide of King Stefan Batory. His support for the Free Election earned him the trust of the nobles, even though he believed in increasing the power of the king. As one of the largest landowners in the Commonwealth, he was closely involved in the development of trade. An educated and intelligent man, he was also a renowned patron of the arts and sciences.

THE WAZA KINGS

From 1587 until 1668 the Polish throne was occupied by three kings of a Swedish dynasty – the Wazas. They were to rule Poland during a period of almost uninterrupted war and civil strife.

The first Waza king was elected by the Polish nobles after the death of King Stefan Batory. He was a Swedish prince, Sigismund Vasa – who in Poland became Zygmunt III Waza. Zygmunt's sons ruled after him, also after winning elections. These were Władysław IV and Jan Kazimierz.

The decision to elect a Swede to the Polish throne had been inspired by plans to combine the countries into a Baltic superpower. It was a dream that never came true. King Zygmunt's Polish mother, Katarzyna Jagiellonka,

had brought him up as a staunch Catholic, an he soon came into conflict with the Lutheran Swedes, who removed him from their throne

The attempts of Zygmunt III and his sons t regain his Swedish crown, as well as the effort of the Swedish branch of the Vasas to create the own Baltic empire, led to a series of wars from 1600 to 1660. Their highpoint was the Swedish invasion of Poland in 1655–57, which was s destructive it became known as the "Deluge".

Besides Sweden, another dangerou opponent of the Polish Commonwealt was emerging in the east – the Gran Duchy of Muscovy, which from the 17t century became known as Russia. Th Russian state had been at war with Polan over control of Livonia since the 1550s. Whe the tyrannical Tsar Ivan IV "the Terrible" die in 1584, Russia descended into chaos. Severa Polish magnates took advantage of the disorde

ZYGMUNT III WAZA (1566–1632)

The son of King Johan III of Sweden, he was elected king of Poland in 1587. He inherited the Swedish throne in 1592, but was soon deposed because of his strongly Roman Catholic views. In Poland his desire to rule as an absolute monarch also brought him into violent conflict with a section of the gentry.

WŁADYSŁAW IV (1595–1648)

The son of Zygmunt III and his first wife, Anna of Habsburg. In 1610 Władysław (Ladislaus) was elected tsar of Russia, but was never crowned. A talented soldier, he did much to modernize the Polish army. He was elected king of Poland after Zygmunt III in 1632, but, unlike his father, was a popular king.

JAN KAZIMIERZ (1609–1672)

Jan Kazimierz (John Casimir) was the son of Zygmunt III's second wife, the Austrian princess Constance. He was elected king after his half-brother's death in 1648. After ruling during 20 years of war and civil turmoil, he abdicated from the throne exhausted in 1668. He died in France four years later.

SIEGE MONEY

In September 1655 a 40,000-strong Swedish army approached Kraków. Church silver was melted down and turned into coins to help pay for the city's defence. The coin shown is a Kraków *Ort*. It has the royal coat of arms with the Polish eagle and Lithuanian knight, and the Waza wheatsheaf at centre. Despite the emergency measures Kraków surrendered after a three-week siege.

o further their private ambitions, and placed an adventurer on the Muscovite throne in 1605. But the inept rule of this "False Dimitri" – who impersonated a dead son of the tsar – led to him being deposed by the Russians. Poland declared war, and in 1610, after a resounding victory at the battle of Klushino (Kłuszyn), a Polish army under Stanisław Żółkiewski marched into Moscow and occupied the Kremlin. Zygmunt III attempted to put his son Władysław on the Russian throne, but refused to compromise on religion. The Orthodox Russians simply would not tolerate the idea of a Catholic tsar, and eventually threw the Polish garrison out of Moscow.

CZĘSTOCHOWA

The holiest site in Poland is the Jasna Góra monastery near Częstochowa. Thanks to massive earthworks it withstood a Swedish siege in 1655. The monastery's almost miraculous defence became a symbol of national resistance when the Swedish war seemed lost. The monastery and its famous Black Madonna icon are the object of pilgrimages to this day.

A NAVAL EXPERIMENT

King Zygmunt III's war with Sweden made it necessary to form a fleet to challenge Swedish supremacy on the Baltic. On 28 November 1627 the fledgling Polish navy of 10 vessels won its greatest victory in an action just off Oliwa near Gdańsk. The Poles captured the Swedish flagship, the *Tigern*, sank a second vessel, the *Solen*, and forced the remaining four Swedish ships to flee. The photo shows a model of the Polish flagship *Rycerz Święty Jerzy* (Knight St. George) which took three hits below the waterline in the battle. Poland's naval experiment ended in 1629 when the ships were loaned to the German Imperial Fleet, and were lost when the Swedes took Wismar in 1632.

LISOWSKI'S COSSACKS

The Polish light horsemen, the "Lisowczyks" – shown in this painting by Józef Brandt – were named after their first colonel, Aleksander Lisowski, who raised them during Russia's "Time of Troubles" in 1611. They fought as mercenaries during the Thirty Years' War in the 1620s, and became feared throughout Europe for their ruthlessness both on and off the battlefield.

Since the 15th century another great power had been growing in the south-east: Ottoman Turkey. Conflict seemed inevitable as Turkey argued with Poland over the control of Moldavia. The dry tinder was further fanned by raids on Poland by subjects of the Turkish sultan – the Tatars, and by raids on Ottoman lands by Polish subjects – the Ukrainian Cossacks*. The war against Turkey began badly in 1620, when at Cecora in Moldavia an expeditionary force under Hetman Żółkiewski was nearly wiped out. The Poles responded in force the following year, and at Chocim on the Moldavian border, with the help of over 30,000 Ukrainian Cossacks, an Ottoman invasion force was repulsed. The Turks agreed peace a few months later.

The Ukrainian Cossacks had been instrumental in turning back the Turks at Chocim, but they were to be the cause of a new war which was to rock Poland to its foundations. The Cossack problem had been growing since the 1569 Union of Lublin, when Ukraine was transferred to Poland from Lithuania. Polish noblemen had set up vast farming estates in the Ukraine, and were making fortunes from the grain trade, while the peasants who worked their land grew poorer and more unhappy. Many sought refuge among the Zaporozhian Cossacks who lived *za porohy*, beyond the rapids of the Dnieper

WARS OF THE POLISH WAZA KINGS				
DATE	SWEDEN	RUSSIA	UKRAINE	TURKEY
1600s	Livonian War: Swedes are defeated at **Kokenhausen** (1601) and **Kircholm** (1605).			
1610s		Żółkiewski defeats Russians at **Kłuszyn** (1610); Poles occupy Moscow (to 1612).	Ukrainian Cossacks raid Turkish Black Sea ports.	
1620s	King Gustav II Adolf of Sweden seizes Polish territory in Livonia (1621) and Prussia (1626). Poland's navy wins its first victory at **Oliwa** (1627); but the army is defeated on land at **Tczew** (1627) and **Górzno** (1629).		Cossack rebellion led by Zhmailo (1625).	Żółkiewski's army is overwhelmed at **Cecora** (1620). Chodkiewicz wins a victory at **Chocim** (1621), so preventing a Turkish invasion of Poland.
1630s	Peace of Stumsdorf (1635) ends the Polish-Swedish War: the Prussian ports are returned to Poland.	The Smolensk War (1633–34):Władysław IV relieves the fortress of **Smolensk** which is besieged by Russian forces.	Cossack rebellions led by Taras Fedorowicz (1630); Sulima (1635); and Pawluk (1637–38).	Hetman Koniecpolski halts a Turkish invasion at **Kamieniec Podolski** (1633–34).
1640s			The Chmielnicki Rebellion begins (1648): Poles are defeated at **Korsuń, Żółte Wody** and **Piławce.** Defence of the fortress of **Zbaraż** (1649).	
1650s	The "Deluge": King Karl X Gustav of Sweden invades Poland (1655). Warsaw and Kraków fall. The war's turning point is the defence of **Jasna Góra** monastery (1655). Three-day battle at **Warsaw** (1656). Sweden's ally Brandenburg obtains Ducal Prussia from Poland (1657).	Tsar Alexis of Russia invades Lithuania (1654–55), and seizes Smolensk and the capital, Vilna (Wilno).	Jan Kazimierz defeats the main Cossack–Tatar army at **Beresteczko** (1651). Chmielnicki annihilates a veteran Polish army at **Batoh** (1652). In revenge, the Poles lay waste to Ukraine (1653–54). At Pereiaslav (1654) the Cossacks swear an oath of loyalty to the Russian tsar.	
1660s	Peace of Oliwa (1660) ends the Swedish war.	Polish victories over the Russians at **Połonka** and **Cudnów** (1660) restore Lithuania to the Commonwealth.	At Andrushovo (1667) Ukraine is formally divided between Poland and Russia.	Turkish attempts to seize the Ukraine are postponed by Sobieski's victory at **Podhajce** (1667).

ŻÓŁKIEWSKI'S LAST STAND

In 1620, at Cecora in Moldavia, a Polish force led by Hetman Stanisław Żółkiewski attempted to prevent a Turkish army from invading Poland. It soon became clear that he was out-matched. Żółkiewski attempted to retreat, but was overrun by the fast-moving Turkish horsemen, and after a heroic last stand was killed, as shown in Witold Piwnicki's painting.

But Żółkiewski's sacrifice had its positive side. Shocked into action, the Seym raised a large army. When the Turks advanced in 1621, they were intercepted at Chocim by Hetman Jan Karol Chodkiewicz. He fought them to a standstill, and forced them to turn back.

* Words marked by an asterisk are explained in the glossary on pages 124–125.

River on an island base known as the "Sich". The number of free Cossacks grew quickly, and soon they had become a powerful military force.

In 1648 the Cossacks revolted under their hetman, Bohdan Chmielnicki. Poland was caught off balance, and several Cossack victories followed. By 1651 the Poles were back on the offensive, and at Beresteczko a huge army led personally by King Jan Kazimierz defeated the combined Cossack–Tatar forces. By 1654 things were looking desperate for Chmielnicki, and he placed Ukraine under Russian protection. Finally, at the treaty of Andrushovo in 1667, all Ukraine east of the Dnieper River was ceded to Russia. A large fertile area of the Polish Commonwealth was lost for ever.

The final result of the destructive Waza kings' wars was a profound weakening of the Polish state. Another disaster had occurred in 1652 in the political arena: the first use of the *Liberum Veto** – the right of deputies to stop the proceedings of the Seym on the grounds that they did not agree with them. This meant that little real business could be done in the Seym. From this point on, Poland's decline seemed inevitable.

THE DELUGE

The many wars fought by Jan Kazimierz brought Poland to the brink of ruin. Large areas were ravaged and depopulated. Most destructive of all was the Swedish occupation of Poland in 1655–57. Many important buildings were destroyed, and works of art and even entire libraries were carted away to Sweden as war booty. Mercenary soldiers – like those in Henryk Pillati's painting – were mainly to blame.

THE COSSACK REVOLT

In 1648 Bohdan Chmielnicki, the Hetman (supreme commander) of the Ukrainian Cossacks, led a revolt against Polish rule in the Ukraine. Unhappy with what he saw as Polish interference in the Orthodox religion, he set up an independent Cossack state in the Ukraine. To strengthen his bargaining position and military strength, Chmielnicki made an alliance with the Tatar leader Tuhai-Bey. Juliusz Kossak's picture shows the meeting of the two leaders.

THE NOBLEMEN'S REPUBLIC

In the early 17th century the Polish–Lithuanian Commonwealth had a population of over 9 million and occupied the greatest territory in its history – 990,000 square kilometres. The period brought prosperity to the magnates, and the estates of several noble families grew greatly in size – notably those of the Zamoyski, Ostrogski, Zasławski, Wiśniowiecki and Lubomirski families.

MICHAŁ KORYBUT WIŚNIOWIECKI (1640–1673)

The son of a famous magnate and soldier, Jeremi Wiśniowiecki, he was elected king in 1669. He proved to be a weak if intelligent monarch, who as one wit remarked, "could speak six languages, but had nothing to say in any of them". His reign was fairly unremarkable.

JAN III SOBIESKI (1629–1696)

The son of a famous soldier, Jakub Sobieski, and grandson of Hetman Żółkiewski, his career path was chosen for him, and he became Grand Hetman in 1668. But his military successes marked him for better things, and he was elected king in 1674. A gifted general, he was also a generous patron of the arts.

JAN III SOBIESKI

Perhaps Poland's most famous king, he was also arguably the country's most talented general. His victory over the Turks at Vienna in 1683 was both the high-point and the end of Poland's career as a major military power.

After Jan Kazimierz abdicated his throne in 1668, the Polish nobility assembled to elect a new king. Tired of the dynastic intrigues of foreign kings, all agreed it was time for a native monarch – a new "Piast". In this way, Michał Korybut Wiśniowiecki became the first elected king of Poland not to be a foreigner.

King Michał was the son of Jeremi Wiśniowiecki (1612–51), a great soldier, famous for his victories over the Ukrainian Cossacks. Michał looked like the ideal person to settle Poland's many problems. Although an intelligent and cultured man, as a king Michał Wiśniowiecki failed to live up to expectations. He was unable to control the machinations of the Polish magnates and proved "little prepared to rule".

King Michał's Poland was a different place from the Poland of only half a century earlier. Weakened by two decades of war against Swedes, Russians and Ukrainian Cossacks, Poland could now defend her borders only with difficulty. It was at this point that the Ottoman Turks saw the opportunity for gain at Poland's expense. In 1672 they seized the crucial border fortress of Kamieniec Podolski, long believed to be impregnable. They went on to ravage Podolia and the Ukraine and seized much of those provinces. Unable to offer proper resistance, the Poles signed the treaty of Buczacz, hoping the Turks would take no more land.

One year later in 1673, a large Polish army was assembled under an as yet little-known commander, Jan Sobieski: the scales began to turn in Poland's favour. At Chocim, Sobieski

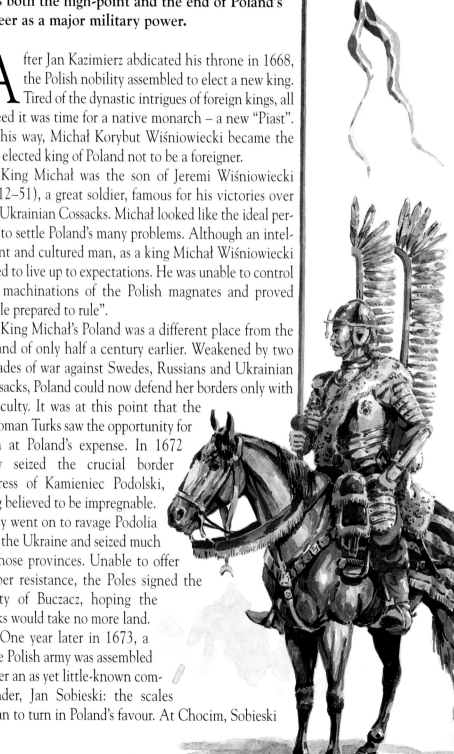

THE SECOND BATTLE OF CHOCIM

On 10 November 1673 the Polish army under Hetman Jan Sobieski stormed Chocim, an old fortress on the Polish-Moldavian border and the site of a victory against the Turks in 1621. Nearly 400 Turkish standards and 40 cannon were captured. It was after this battle that Sobieski began to be feared in Turkey and admired in Poland.

victory before the gates of Vienna. The Imperial capital was saved, the Turkish menace at last defeated. Sobieski became an international hero, and Poland received the thanks and praise of all Europe.

King Jan III's military talents continued to pay dividends in the Turkish wars of the later 1680s and 1690s, and the peace signed at Karlowitz in 1699 returned to Poland most of the territories lost to Turkey in the 1670s. But these successes had a high cost. Sobieski failed to put adequate efforts into dealing with his ambitious neighbours Sweden, Russia and Brandenburg–Prussia. He signed an alliance with France, hoping it would help Poland recover Ducal Prussia, but this was not enough. He also failed to reform the rusty machinery of state, and by the end of his reign this had all but seized up. These oversights were to leave Poland as little more than a victim on the international stage in the 18th century.

inflicted a humiliating defeat on the Turks. Shortly after the battle King Michał died and, in the royal elections which followed in 1674 Sobieski was swept to power as King Jan III – only the second native Pole to be elected king of Poland.

Sobieski's greatest moment came in 1683, when another Turkish army of 100,000 men laid siege to the Imperial capital, Vienna. After desperate pleas from the pope and the Habsburg emperor, Leopold II, to "save Christian Europe from the rising tide of Islam", Sobieski marched for Austria with an army of 30,000 Poles. Once near Vienna, King Jan III was appointed commander-in-chief of the combined Polish and German Imperial armies. On 12 September 1683 he led the allies to a great

THE RELIEF OF VIENNA

The battle of Vienna took place on 12 September 1683. For much of the day Polish infantry fought to clear the wooded hills around Vienna from Turks. Only towards evening had enough space been made on the Vienna plain for the Polish-Austrian army to deploy. On a signal from Sobieski, the cavalry led by 3,000 Polish "winged" hussars smashed through the Turkish army led by Kara Mustafa, and poured into the Ottoman camp. The Turks fled in panic; Vienna was saved. After the battle, King Jan III rode into Vienna to a tumultuous reception (as shown in Juliusz Kossak's painting). He described the event in a letter to his beloved French wife Marysieńka: "Today I was in the city, which would have held out five more days, no more ... All the common people kissed my hands, my feet, my clothes; others only touched me, saying: 'Ach, let us kiss so valiant a hand!'"

THE WINGED HUSSARS

The legendary hussars were responsible for many of Poland's great victories. Each hussar wore metal plate armour and his main weapon was the eastern lance (*kopia*), which broke on striking an enemy. In close combat the hussar reached for one of his two swords – either the *koncerz* designed for piercing mail armour, or a sabre for slashing strokes. The "wings" worn on the back or on the saddle are still a mystery. They did not, as is often claimed, make a rustling noise during the charge. Contemporaries believed it was their spectacular sight alone that frightened enemy horses, "who were unused to seeing such visions".

A NOBLEMAN'S PARADISE?

Despite her political problems and incessant wars, Poland in the 17th and early 18th centuries developed a unique nobleman's culture. Two words sum up this remarkable artistic flowering: baroque and Sarmatism.

The baroque movement was born in Italy at the start of the 17th century. The word derives from the Spanish *barueco*, meaning a pearl of irregular shape. In many ways the term sums up Polish culture in this period: it was elegant and rich, but somehow fundamentally warped.

The centre of the Polish baroque was undoubtedly Warsaw. The city had become Poland's capital in place of Kraków in 1596, largely because King Zygmunt III wanted to be located closer to the heart of the three realms of Poland, Lithuania and Sweden. Warsaw was then just a small town, but it grew rapidly. The Warsaw Royal Castle (*below*) was rebuilt between 1598 and 1618 as the official residence of the Waza kings, and soon became a centre for baroque culture – the meeting place of artists, musicians and actors. The interior was lined with artistic wonders: oil paintings by Dutch and Italian masters, marble sculptures and gilded woodwork

CHURCH BAROQUE
Of the many Polish buildings erected in the baroque style, the parish church in Poznań (built 1651–1732) is among the most lavish. The interior is decorated in the ornate style so typical of baroque – with dozens of sculptures, pictures and gilded ornaments – giving a suitable setting for Holy Mass. Despite the violence of recent history, many such marvels of the Polish baroque have survived intact.

(most of them, unfortunately, destroyed or looted during the Swedish invasion of 1655–57.) Seeing the opulence of the royal court, the magnates began to build and embellish their own country and town houses in a similar manner.

Before long the baroque style had spread to church architecture, and had percolated down even to the modest homes of the lesser nobles.

KING ZYGMUNT'S COLUMN
Warsaw's best known landmark is located in front of the Royal Castle. Designed by Constantino Tencalla, it was erected in 1643 by Władysław IV in memory of his father Zygmunt III Waza.

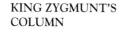

Linked closely with baroque was another 17th-century trend – Sarmatism. This uniquely Polish phenomenon arose because the noblemen believed they were descended from an ancient tribe of horse warriors – the Sarmatians. In reality, they had little to do with this nomadic people who had ruled lands north of the Black Sea until the 4th century AD; but thanks to the Sarmatian myth, Polish nobility developed a taste for Eastern fashions and a love of swift Arab horses. With his shaven Asian-nomad hairstyle, a sabre at his side, and his devil-may-care attitude, there was a little of the Tatar in every Polish nobleman.

Sarmatism also had its less attractive side. It encouraged a sense of superiority over the peasants, who were not of "Sarmatian" blood, and so could be ruthlessly exploited, much as the Tatars exploited the *yassyr* or prisoners they captured on campaign. The nobles began to see their lives as charmed, and the "Golden Freedom" as theirs by right. Sarmatism created a pride in all things Polish, but it also bred a dangerous form of arrogance which was to lead to Poland's downfall.

KRASIŃSKI PALACE

The architect of one of Poland's most splendid baroque palaces was a polonized Dutchman, Tilman van Gameren (Gamerski).

WILANÓW PALACE

Transformed from a small country house between 1681 and 1696, Wilanów Palace became a residence literally "fit for a king" – namely, Jan III Sobieski. The chief architect was Augustyn Locci, a Pole of Italian origin who was also King Jan III's secretary and his advisor on artistic matters.

A NOBLEMAN'S MEMOIRS

Poland's best-known 17th--century memoir writer was Jan Chryzostom Pasek. It is clear that he was a bigoted, hard-drinking, argumentative raconteur, yet he is amusing and strangely charismatic. His memoirs were written in Polish interwoven with Latin phrases, a style known as "macaronism". Here is a fairly typical extract:

"THE YEAR OF OUR LORD 1679

The first Seym of the year in Lithuania was held in Grodno. The Lithuanian gentlemen, overruling our objections, forced through a resolution to hold two Seym meetings in Poland, one after the other, and the third in Lithuania, travelling to which is very *molestum* [burdensome] for us, and it will be in *perpetuitas* now that it has come into usage. Our army this year, being encamped at Trembowla summer and winter long, were no longer soldiers but farmers; they cultivated the land, sowing, ploughing, and had plenty of everything, just like at home. All that was missing were their wives."

Like other Polish noblemen, Pasek wore clothing inspired by the Orient. The main garment was a *kontusz*, which was worn over a tight-fitting *żupan*, with a silk sash at the waist. In the 18th century this became the national costume.

Polish nobleman in 18th-century national costume

THE SAXON KINGS

During the first half of the 18th century the Polish–Lithuanian Commonwealth was ruled by two elected kings of the Wettin dynasty from Saxony in Germany. Their reigns were marked by a severe downturn in Poland's fortunes.

AUGUST II "THE STRONG" (1670–1733)

The elector (ruler) of Saxony as Friedrich August of the Wettin dynasty, he ruled Poland as King August II from 1697–1704, and again from 1710–1733.

AUGUST III (1696–1763)

The son of August II. In 1733, with the support of Russia and Austria, he took the Polish throne. He was less talented than his father and made little attempt to intervene in Polish politics.

Two Saxon kings ruled Poland in turn – August II and his son August III. Happy in their elegant palaces in Saxony, they left the Polish noblemen to do more or less as they pleased. The magnates became ever more quarrelsome, selfish and wealthy. Some raised their own armies, and even conducted independent relations with foreign powers. In the increasing lawlessness, the Seym was broken up time after time, and any attempts to reform the government were met with a type of legal rebellion, known as a Confederation*. And it was this state of near anarchy, so comfortable for the wealthy noblemen, that was known as the "Golden Freedom".

While Poland was paralysed in this way, her neighbours – Russia, Austria and Prussia – were becoming ever more powerful. Taking advantage of the self-indulgence of the magnates, they conspired to ensure that the "Polish anarchy" continued. Poland's army was now hopelessly outnumbered and outclassed and could no longer defend the borders. During the Great Northern War of 1700–21, Poland was repeatedly violated by Swedish, Saxon and Russian armies. They devastated the countryside and occupied all the major cities. At Kliszów (1702), one of many battles fought on Polish soil, even the famous "winged" hussars ran away from a smaller enemy force, demonstrating just how low Poland's military power had fallen.

In 1704 King Karl XII of Sweden defeated August II's armies and placed the Polish crown on the head of

TREATY OF THE THREE BLACK EAGLES

In 1732 three states whose national emblem was a black eagle – Russia, Prussia and Austria – signed an agreement concerning the succession to the Polish throne, hoping to prevent the election of a Pole. Each of the signatories was becoming a modern nation state, with a large army and an efficient treasury. Meanwhile, Poland had an obsolete army, and an economy in ruins. Effectively, the "Treaty of the Three Black Eagles" prevented Poland's citizens from determining their own future.

TOKEN OF LOVE

August II, called "the Strong", was famous for his amorous adventures and his many mistresses. In 1708 he issued a series of coins including this splendid *thaler* (with a stated value of 32 *groschen*) in honour of a favourite mistress, Countess Cosel.

* Words marked by an asterisk are explained in the glossary on pages 124–125.

Stanisław Leszczyński. Within a few years the Swedes were defeated, and the throne was restored to August II. When August II attempted to strengthen his position in Poland he provoked a rebellion among the nobles – the Tarnogród Confederation (1715). The Russian tsar*, Peter the Great, saw his chance. In the guise of a peace-maker, he got the factions to sign a truce. He then sent Russian soldiers into the "Silent Seym" of 1717. Frightened into silence, the Polish deputies signed away many of their powers and gave the tsar the legal right to intervene in Polish affairs. It was a body-blow to Polish independence. Two centuries of Russian domination were to follow.

On the death of August II in 1733 another international conflict erupted. Stanisław Leszczyński was re-elected king of Poland with the support of France, but Russia and Austria declared in favour of the old Saxon king's son. After three years of bitter fighting, they

installed him as King August III. This, the so-called War of Polish Succession, demonstrated that Poland was no longer in control of her own destiny.

STANISŁAW LESZCZYŃSKI (1677–1766)

Appointed *wojewoda* of Poznań in 1699, he twice became king of Poland: from 1704 to 1709 after the Swedes had defeated August II, and from 1733 to 1736 when he won the majority of votes in the royal election. One of Poland's more enlightened monarchs, he was a great patron of the arts. After losing his crown the second time, he emigrated to France where he received the duchy of Lorraine from King Louis XV.

HOME OF THE SAXON KINGS

August II and August III were rulers (electors) of Saxony, as well as kings of Poland. Their Saxon electorship was heredi-tary, and gave the powers to govern Saxony efficiently. All attempts at reforming Poland along Saxon lines proved impossible, and the two states retained separate armies and governments. The Wettin kings seldom went to Poland, and generally preferred to stay in Dresden, the capital of Saxony, content in their elegant lifestyle among some of the most splendid palaces of the age (*as shown in Canaletto's painting*). Much of the colossal cost of building these palaces was obtained from income received in Poland.

SAXON DECADENCE

Black clouds had long been forming over Poland, but the true collapse began in the first half of the 18th century during the misrule of the Saxon kings. The country was seen abroad as opulent and free, yet in uncontrollable decay.

The life of the typical Polish nobleman of the Saxon period was comfortable. He interested himself more with the affairs of his locality than with the fate of his country at large. Much of his time was spent making merry. The slogans of the age were: "Under the Saxon king, eat, drink and loosen your belt", and "Keep up appearances, at all costs". It was quite normal to spend a fortune on beautiful horses and elegant clothing, and to get into horrendous debt. It was also common for a nobleman's estate (which had taken generations to build up) to be ruined and the peasants working his lands to be reduced to abject poverty.

In these circumstances, it is little wonder that many men of "noble birth" were unable to read or write. The few who, despite the distractions, still received an education usually ended up in schools run by Jesuits. The Jesuits concentrated on teaching Latin and the Catholic religion in its most extreme form. There was little time for Polish language, history or geography. Most noblemen left such schools ignorant of the world at large and openly hostile to other religions. Unfamiliar happenings were explained in terms of magic and witchcraft or as "acts of God". Many innocent persons, especially women, were tried for witchcraft and burnt at the stake. The dislike of Protestants and Jews also began to increase. In 1717 new laws forbade the construction of new places of worship for all dissenting creeds and made it illegal to repair those that already existed. The age of Poland's famous religious tolerance had come to an end.

Few good things can be said about the progress of Polish science and literature in this period. Most Polish men and women read little except prayer books and the Bible. Memoir writing, which had been popular in the 17th century, began to decline. One notable exception

THE DECLINE OF THE BAROQUE

The reigns of the Saxon kings saw the decline of baroque architecture and the beginning a new courtly style – rococo. Often seen as the last phase of baroque, rococo was characterized by lightness and elegance, and a love of detail and rich decoration. The courtyard of the Poznań Jesuit College was built between 1701 and 1733, partly in late baroque style, and was reworked in the following century.

AT THE STAKE

Women accused of witchcraft were still burnt at the stake until the 18th century. Poland became increasingly intolerant of "heretics", mostly due to the stultifying influence of the Jesuits.

THE SAXON GARDEN

Opened to the general public in 1727, the "Saxon Garden" was the first park in Warsaw, and is still open to this day.

was the work of Father Jędrzej Kitowicz, who wrote a remarkable and meticulous account of everyday life in the Saxon age (*see panel, below right*).

Fortunately, under the second Saxon king, August III, several Poles began to see the need for change. In this spirit the exiled king Stanisław Leszczyński wrote a pamphlet entitled *A Free Voice Ensuring Freedom* (1749); it was one of the most important political tracts of the age.

Meanwhile, Stanisław Konarski promoted political change, starting with reform of the backward education system. In 1747 the brothers Józef Andrzej and Andrzej Stanisław Załuski opened their library to scholars; soon it had become one of the largest public libraries in Europe. The activities of such patriots were to increase greatly in the second half of the 18th century.

FUNERAL PORTRAITS

The 17th and early 18th centuries saw a uniquely Polish type of painting among the nobility.

Small head-and-shoulders portraits of the deceased were painted in oil on a tin plate, which was attached to the funeral casket.

STANISŁAW KONARSKI (1700–1773)

Influential educational reformer and political activist. In 1740, after tireless efforts, he opened a school – the Collegium Nobilium – in Warsaw, for men of noble birth, intending it to rival the narrow schooling of the Jesuits. Studies were to take seven years, with the stress on Polish and foreign languages, natural sciences and geography. Polish history was also seen as a key part of a patriotic upbringing.

WOODEN CHURCHES

Many more wooden churches were built in Poland than stone ones. The church at Wełna, not far from Rogoźno near Poznań, was built in 1727, and is a good example of this distinctly eastern European style of wooden architecture.

THE NOBLEMAN'S CUSTOMS

Father Jędrzej Kitowicz's book, *A Description of Customs in the Reign of August III*, gives a unique insight into the Polish nobleman's life in the mid-18th century. Written with great attention to detail, it covers everything from military fashions to cooking recipes. Much of Kitowicz's work criticized the decadent habits of men in positions of power. The following extract gives some idea of the chaos of a Polish local government meeting (*seymik**).

"The lords and powerful nobles were well entertained at the *seymiks* with choice delicacies and good drinks, especially Hungarian wine, which wherever they were given more and better, there the greater was the turnout. The lesser noblemen […] had separate tables, in various hostelries, and in summer out

in orchards or in courtyards under shelters. […] The food for the lesser noblemen was not elegant; typically meat: beef, pork, lamb, any kind of chicken, goose or turkey; all roasted or boiled and well peppered, salty and sour, to encourage the thirst for alcohol. […]
At length the gluttony was halted, while they were still conscious and able to do the work of the *seymik*, which took place in a church or cemetery, to which they were led by clerks, who told them which proposals to support and which to obstruct."

A ROCOCO PALACE

The home of the Sułkowski princes at Rydzyna was built between 1741 and 1750. The façade and interiors were in the elegant new rococo style.

THE LAST KING OF POLAND

In 1764 Empress Catherine the Great of Russia supported the election of her former lover Stanisław August Poniatowski to the Polish throne. She was surprised when, rather than acting as her obedient servant, he attempt to overthrow Russia's domination and helped to introduce Europe's most modern Constitution.

After the death of King August III of the Saxon dynasty, a new "Piast" candidate came forward for the Polish crown: Stanisław August Poniatowski. He was elected with the help of troops sent by Catherine II of Russia in 1764. The Russian empress believed she would easily be able to control the new king of Poland. He quickly surprised her by his independence of mind, and his desire to reform the machinery of state.

When, in 1765, the Seym was presented with a bill to abolish the *Liberum Veto*, alarm bells began to sound in St Petersburg and Berlin. The project was quickly quashed. To hamper further attempts at reform, Prussia and Russia began to sow disorder in Poland. Most Polish nobles were Catholics and were against persons of Orthodox and Protestant faiths acquiring equal civic rights. When gossip spread that the king planned to grant such rights, in line with Russian and Prussian demands, Poland descended into chaos. Armies of noblemen gathered, and Russian troops marched into Poland. In 1768 at Bar in Podolia, a Confederation* declared war on the king, in defence of religion and the nobles' privileges. An absurd and pointless armed conflict broke out. Finally, in 1772, claiming that Poland was clearly incapable of governing itself, Prussia, Austria and Russia signed a treaty awarding themselves 30 percent, in total, of Poland's territory: it was the First Partition of Poland.

In a further attempt to keep Poland weak, the Russians sponsored the setting up in 1772 of a Permanent

STANISŁAW AUGUST PONIATOWSKI (1732–1798)

After serving as Poland's representative at the Russian court from 1755 to 1758, he was elected king of Poland with the support of Empress Catherine II in 1764. Not content to be her lackey he sided with the "Patriotic Party" during the Great Seym, and helped create the Constitution of 3 May 1791. However, realizing the ultimate futility of opposing the Russians, he sided from July 1792 with the Constitution's opponents, the Targowica Confederates, and in 1795, after the Third Partition, he abdicated from the throne. During his reign he was a great patron of literature, science and art. The gold coin portrait was designed by the court medallist Johann Philipp Holzhäusser who worked at the Warsaw mint.

THE CONFEDERATION OF BAR

The Bar Confederates saw themselves as defenders of the "Golden Freedom", but wished to halt the meddling of foreign powers in Polish affairs, especially Russia. One of the most distinguished of the Confederation partisans was Kazimierz Pułaski (shown here in Józef Chełmoński's painting at the defence of Częstochowa). After taking the monastery of Jasna Góra in 1770, the Bar Confederates held off Russian attacks until 1772. After the collapse of the Bar Confederation, Pułaski emigrated to America, where he fought in the War of Independence against Britain.

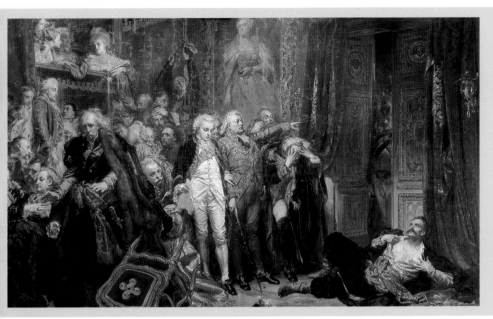

TADEUSZ REJTAN

As a political gesture the Seym of 1773 had to ratify the treaty of Partition which allowed Austria, Prussia and Russia to annex large areas of Polish territory. The majority of Seym members had been bribed to sign. In a desperate attempt to stop them the deputy for Nowogródek, Tadeusz Rejtan, threw himself on the floor, tore open his clothes, and begged to be killed rather than see his colleagues sign so shameful a document. The dramatic scene was later reconstructed in a famous painting by Jan Matejko.

STANISŁAW STASZIC (1755–1826)

One of the most outspoken patriots of his day. Famous for translating Homer's *Iliad*, he wrote tracts calling for the reform of Poland's social, economic and political ills. He continued to be active after the Polish state had been partitioned away.

Council, with strictly limited powers. Thanks to King Stanisław August's intervention, however, the body soon became an remarkably efficient instrument of state. Paradoxically, the Permanent Council was able to introduce reforms in the army, the treasury and the legislative system which would have been impossible during ordinary deliberations of the Seym.

More fundamental reforms, however, required the Seym's approval, which was unlikely while the Partitioning Powers were pulling all the strings. The opportunity came in 1788 when the international situation provided distractions. Russia was at war with Turkey and Sweden; Prussia was openly hostile to Russia and Austria; meanwhile France was on the verge of its Revolution. The Seym which began deliberations in late 1788 cast caution to the wind; it voted an increase in the size of the army, and then abolished the Permanent Council. From the beginning a "Patriotic Party" managed to outmanoeuvre conservative elements. The "Great Seym" was eventually to sit for four years (1788–92) working on its programme of reform. Undoubtedly the key achievement was the declaration of Poland's historic first constitution on 3 May 1791.

The new Constitution did not pass unnoticed for long. The Russians secretly assembled Polish noblemen who were opposed to reform, and at Targowica got them

THE CONSTITUTION OF 3 MAY 1791

The crowning achievement of the Great Seym of 1788–92 was the declaration of the Constitution of 3 May (above). It abolished the evils of the "Polish anarchy", introduced a hereditary monarchy, and for the first time gave the peasants the political protection of the state. The new Constitution was a concrete sign that Poland had finally chosen the road of reform and progress.

OLD POLAND

declare another Confederation. Four days later on 18 May 1792 Russian troops marched into Poland.

The war began well for the Poles. General Józef Poniatowski – the king's nephew and a later marshal of France – distinguished himself at the battle of Zieleńce (18 June), while at the battle of Dubienka (18 July) another general, Tadeusz Kościuszko, continued his rise to fame. But Russia's armed strength was overwhelming, and her eventual victory was inevitable. When the war ended in 1793, punishment came swiftly: Russia presided over the Second Partition of Poland in co-operation with Prussia.

In 1794 Kościuszko was provoked into leading a second insurrection against the Russians. He won a remarkable victory at Racławice in April; but nothing could save Poland from the superior might of her enemies. At the battle of Maciejowice, Kościuszko was wounded and captured, and in November 1794 Warsaw fell after a heroic defence. The Insurrection collapsed.

In 1795 Austria, Russia and Prussia signed a treaty on the Third Partition, and Poland disappeared completely from the map of Europe. The selfishness and pride of the nobles had, over the centuries, repeatedly brought Poland close to ruin. Now, just as the Poles were seeing the error of their ways, the struggle came to an abrupt end.

KOŚCIUSZKO'S SCYTHEMEN

When the 1794 Insurrection broke out, Kościuszko realized that his only chance of winning was to mobilize the entire population, which meant organizing the peasants into militias. To cut costs many were issued with simple uniforms recut from peasant clothing, and with weapons improvised by straightening out farm scythes. Despite their un-military appearance, Kościuszko's scythemen – the *Kosynierzy* – soon earned themselves a fearsome reputation.

KOŚCIUSZKO'S OATH

The annulment of the Constitution of 3rd May and the Second Partition in 1793 provoked a fresh insurrection. At its head was Tadeusz Kościuszko, a veteran of America's War of Independence (1775–83). On 24 March 1794, in Kraków's town square, Kościuszko swore, as the *Naczelnik* (Leader) of Poland's armed forces, to evict the armies of the Partitioning Powers.

BATTLE OF RACŁAWICE

On 4 April 1794 the first battle of the Kościuszko Insurrection took place at Racławice near Kraków. The action was largely decided by 320 of Kościuszko's peasant militiamen, who charged a key Russian artillery battery with their scythes alone. Especially distinguished was Wojciech Bartos, who stopped a Russian gun from firing with his cap (as in this detail of the Racławice Panorama). For his bravery Bartos was made an officer and granted the noble name "Głowacki".

THE PRAGA MASSACRE

Despite Polish victories early in the Kościuszko Insurrection, the Russians responded with massive force, and the end was only a matter of time. The last heroic act of the Insurrection was the siege of Warsaw. The final Russian attack on the Praga suburb took place on 4 November 1794. After Praga's fall, Russian soldiers massacred the civilians in their houses, as shown in Aleksander Orłowski's painting made soon after the dreadful event.

THE PARTITIONS OF POLAND

— Poland's borders before the Partitions

	Prussia	Russia	Austria
1st Partition (1772)			
2nd Partition (1793)			
3rd Partition (1795)			

ELECTED KINGS OF POLAND

HENRYK WALEZY (1573–1574)

STEFAN BATORY (1576–1586)

ZYGMUNT III WAZA (1587–1632)

WŁADYSŁAW IV WAZA (1632–1648)

JAN KAZIMIERZ WAZA (1648–1668)

MICHAŁ KORYBUT WIŚNIOWIECKI (1669–1673)

JAN III SOBIESKI (1674–1696)

AUGUST II THE STRONG (1697–1704, 1709–1733)

STANISŁAW LESZCZYŃSKI (1704–1709, 1733–1736)

AUGUST III (1733–1763)

STANISŁAW AUGUST PONIATOWSKI (1764–1795)

THE POLISH ENLIGHTENMENT

The intellectual movement known as the Enlightenment transformed 18th century Europe. The new ideas flowered quite late in Poland, in the 1770s, but by the end of the century Polish culture was once more in full bloom.

The ideal citizen of the new "enlightened" age had an all-round education, was sensitive to beauty, refined in manners, and knowledgeable in matters of art and literature. Such concepts remained largely alien in Poland for much of the 18th century, while small-mindedness, drunkenness and over-inflated pride held sway among the Polish nobility. Such problems remained intractable until schooling ceased to be a luxury.

Poland's school system – the backbone of any country's culture – had been allowed to decline in the early decades of the 18th century. When King Stanisław August Poniatowski came to power, he personally began to see that the situation was remedied. In 1765 he set up the "School of Chivalry" – Poland's first military school, which trained the elite of society, and not just in matters of war. Eight years later the King oversaw the creation of the National Education Commission, one of the first of its type in the world. A "Society for Elementary Books" was also established, and quickly began to produce some of the best textbooks in Europe.

The new appreciation of intellectual life saw rapid improvements in the new mass media, and created a number of outstanding creative personalities: Franciszek Bohomolec, editor of the *Monitor* newspaper; Adam Naruszewicz, author of the *History of the Polish Nation*; Ignacy Krasicki, author of satires and poems such as *Myszeida* and *Monachomachia*; Julian Ursyn Niemcewicz, historian, deputy at the Great Seym and co-founder of the newspaper *Gazeta Narodowa i Obca*, which quickly rivalled the top French and English newspapers in quality; and last but not least, Wojciech Bogusławski, actor and playwright, who oversaw the rebirth of national theatre.

The arts benefited greatly from the last king of Poland's careful patronage. As well as sponsoring Poles to

King Stanisław August Poniatowski by Marcello Bacciarelli

travel abroad, he drew a circle of internationally famous artists to Poland. Among them were the Italian painter Marcello Bacciarelli and Bernardo Belotto called "Canaletto", and the king's court architect, Domenico Merlini. Warsaw was soon graced with dozens of grand new buildings: churches, palaces, banks as well as town houses, built in late-baroque and neo-classical styles. The Royal Castle was renovated, and decorated with new paintings and sculptures, while at Łazienki, south of Warsaw, a new suburban royal residence was built, with its splendidly scenic "Palace upon the Water".

ROYAL STYLE

The throne room and chapel of Warsaw's Royal Castle were renovated in the latest style by Domenico Merlini.

ARCHITECTURE OF THE ENLIGHTENMENT

The splendid royal residence at Łazienki, known as the Palace upon the Water, was the work of Domenico Merlini and Jan Chrystian Kamsetzer. It was the venue for the "Thursday lunches" to which King Stanisław August invited famous literati of the era. Łazienki is also the site of the "Theatre on the Island" where performances are still held today.

The Primate's Palace in Warsaw, the residence of the head of the Church, is a splendid example of the neo-classical style which became popular towards the end of the 18th century.

The palace complex at Czerniejewo is another fine neo-classical building. The two-story structure was erected between 1770 and 1780, and has two small wings and a four-column portico.

CANALETTO'S WARSAW

Thanks to Bernardo Belotto called Canaletto we have a good idea how Warsaw (here Miodowa Street) looked in the late 18th century.

IGNACY KRASICKI
(1735–1801)

Without doubt the most illustrious writer of the Enlightenment in Poland. He wrote plays, novels, poems, fables, histories and biographies, and still had time to help edit the weekly newspaper, *Monitor*, which was patterned on the English *Spectator*.

A great supporter of reform and of "modern ways" he disliked ignorance more than anything else. Although holding the office of bishop of Warmia, he openly criticized the stupidity and idleness of much of the clergy. One of his most famous works *Monachomachia* (The War of the Monks), concerned the petty rivalries of the various religious orders.

THE "SCHOOL OF CHIVALRY"

The first non-religious college in Poland (established 1765) was far more than just a school for war. Many of the great figures of Poland's struggle for independence passed through as cadets – not least: Tadeusz Kościuszko, Julian Ursyn Niemcewicz and Jakub Jasiński.

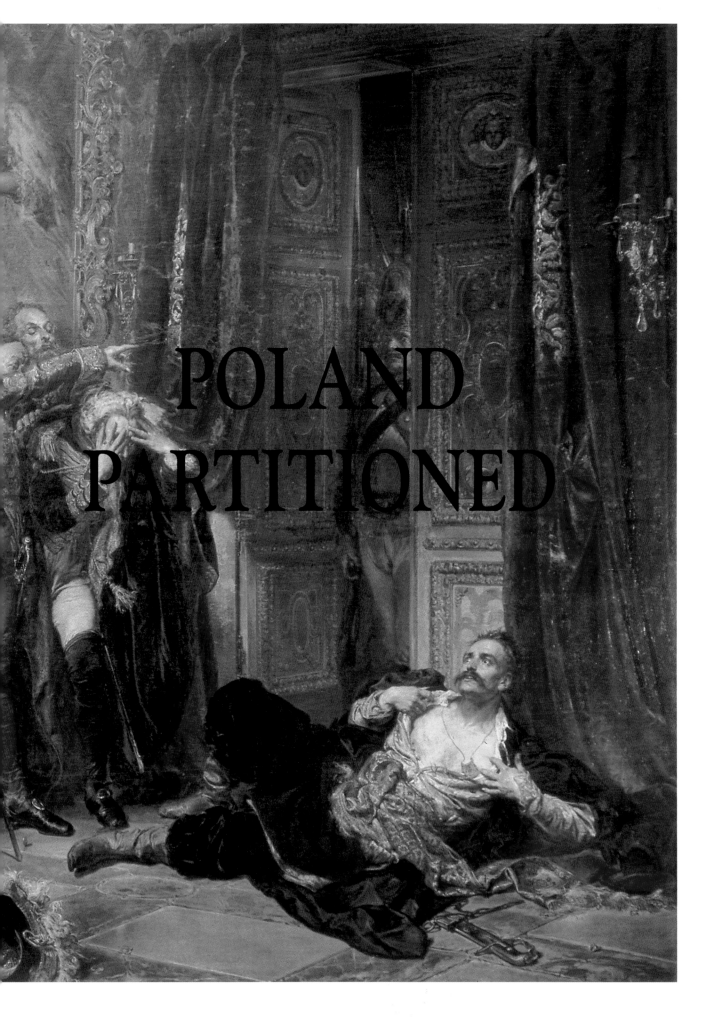
POLAND
PARTITIONED

IN FRENCH SERVICE – DĄBROWSKI'S LEGIONS

After the Third Partition of 1795 Poland ceased to exist as a sovereign nation. For the next 123 years the country disappeared from the map of Europe. The search for independence forced many Poles to go abroad, especially to France.

While Poland was suffering the trauma of the Partitions, France was also undergoing great transformations which had began with the 1789 revolution. By lending support to the French in their hour of need, Polish patriots hoped the French would, in turn, help Poland achieve independence. Among the Poles who travelled to Paris was General Jan Henryk Dąbrowski, who went to the aid of another Polish activist Józef Wybicki. They suggested creating a Polish army in France, but the French revolutionary authorities at first refused to approve this.

A new opportunity appeared when Napoleon Bonaparte began his rise to power. In 1796 he was in command of French troops stationed in Lombardy in northern Italy. On 9 January 1797 he gave permission for the levying of a Polish "Legion" under General Dąbrowski to assist in the war against Austria. The troops had to wear Italian epaulettes and French cockades, but were authorized to wear Polish uniforms and to use Polish as their language of command. Almost immediately 3,500 Poles signed up, many of them Polish prisoners of war captured from the Imperial Austrian army. By the summer of 1797 Dąbrowski had successfully raised a second Polish legion and was in command of about 7,000 soldiers. By 1799 a third formation had been formed: known as the Danube Legion, it was led by General Karol Kniaziewicz, and was composed of infantry, cavalry and artillery.

The atmosphere of the legions was egalitarian and friendly. Organization was democratic, corporal punishment was forbidden, and in free time officers taught their soldiers the basics of Polish history and how to read and write. The legionnaires marched to a patriotic song, especially composed for them by Józef Wybicki: "Jeszcze Polska nie umarła, póki my żyjemy" (Poland had not yet perished, so long as we still live). Known at the time as *Dąbrowski's Mazurka*, the song later became the Polish national anthem.

The Legions soon proved themselves to be a valuable part of Napoleon's assets in Italy. They played a decisive role in the battle of Civita-Castellana in 1798, and took heavy losses at the Trebbia (1799) and Hohenlinden (1800). But events soon took a turn for the worse.

DĄBROWSKI IN ITALY
Jan Henryk Dąbrowski was the mastermind behind the Polish

Legions. The painting by January Suchodolski shows him arriving in Italy.

JAN HENRYK DĄBROWSKI (1755–1818)
The founder of the Polish Legions. After serving in the Saxon army he switched to Polish service, and distinguished himself in the 1794 Insurrection. After his involvement with the Legions in Italy, he returned to Wielkopolska in 1806 to organize another army. After Prince Józef Poniatowski's death he became the supreme

commander of Poland's troops. He left interesting memoirs of his eventful life.

The 1801 peace treaty between Austria and France made no mention of the "Polish Question". In disgust, many Poles resigned from the Legions, and discipline crumbled. It was becoming clear that Napoleon intended to use his Polish troops as little more than mercenaries. They were to fight under French standards, with little acknowledgement that they were Poles and not Frenchmen. In 1802 and 1803 Dąbrowski's disheartened soldiers were treated with contempt by the French authorities: two Legions, renumbered as the 113th and 114th *Demi-brigades* of the French line, were forced onto ships at gunpoint and sent to the West Indies to put down a negro slave rebellion. In the fever-ridden swamps of Haiti most of them died. Many went over to help the rebels; hundreds more rotted away on British prison ships; barely 300 survivors, many suffering from tropical diseases, returned home many years later.

Despite such disappointments, Dąbrowski's Legions had enormous importance. For Poles at home and in exile abroad they were a concrete sign of hope for the future. About 33,000 Poles served in the Legions at one time or another, and when the Duchy of Warsaw was set up in 1807 there were still 4,000 Polish troops in Italy. Even if the Legions did not achieve Polish independence as originally hoped, they provided a pool of officers and men trained in the latest techniques, which was to be a valuable resource for the future.

JÓZEF WYBICKI (1747–1822)

A participant in the Bar Confederation in 1768, he was active in the National Education Commission from 1777. He emigrated to France after the collapse of the Kościuszko Insurrection and was co-founder of the Polish Legions in Italy. In 1797 he wrote the words to the Polish national anthem.

NAPOLEON BONAPARTE (1769–1821)

Born in Corsica and trained as an artillery officer, Napoleon soon displayed his prodigious energy. He took command of French forces in Italy in 1796, declared himself First Consul of France in 1799, and crowned himself Emperor in 1804. A brilliant military commander, he turned France into the dominant European power, until defeated in the 1812 Moscow campaign and at Waterloo in 1815.

Napoleon had an obvious sympathy for the Poles (not least his mistress Maria Walewska), but he clearly exploited Polish patriotism for his own ends. Even so, most Poles saw Napoleon as their main hope for achieving independence.

THE POLISH ANTHEM

*"Poland has not yet perished
So long as we still live.
What foreign force has seized,
We at swordpoint shall retrieve.*

*March, march, Dąbrowski!
From Italy to Poland.
Under your command,
Let us rejoin our nation."*

Composed by Józef Wybicki in 1797 the words referred to Dąbrowski's Legions. Known at first as Dąbrowski's *Mazurka*, the song became hugely popular. From 1831 it became the national anthem, and from 1927 the official state anthem.

a soldier of the Polish Legions

THE DUCHY OF WARSAW

In 1806 Napoleon defeated the Prussian army and marched into Prussia. Wanting Polish troops to strengthen his forces, he re-established Poland as a semi-independent power, and named it the Duchy of Warsaw.

Napoleon had great dreams of conquest. After defeating the Austrians at Austerlitz (1805) and the Prussians at Jena (1806), he marched east towards the former territories of Poland. Needing to raise more troops for his campaigns, he ordered the founders of the Polish Legions – Wybicki and Dąbrowski – to Berlin, hoping to benefit from the esteem these men were held in by their countrymen. In November 1806 the two officers entered Poznań, amid popular jubilation, and began levying soldiers for Napoleon in Wielkopolska.

The Emperor marched on to Warsaw, and on 14 January 1807 set up a Ruling Commission to govern the liberated Polish territories. The body's president was Stanisław Małachowski, who had been Marshal of the Seym before the Partitions. Command of the new Polish army was entrusted to General Józef Poniatowski. Three new divisions were raised, initially under generals Poniatowski (1st), Zajączek (2nd) and Dąbrowski (3rd), numbering 30,000 men in all.

In June 1807 Napoleon inflicted a crushing defeat on the Russians at the battle of Friedland. A month later on 7 July he signed a treaty at Tilsit imposing harsh terms on Russia. On the strength of the treaty, Napoleon created a new Polish state known as the Duchy of Warsaw. It included only a portion of the old Polish lands – namely the territories taken by Prussia in the Second and Third Partitions, along with Warsaw, Toruń and Poznań – an area of 104,000 square kilometres with about 2.7 million inhabitants. The king of Saxony, Friedrich August Wettin, became the titular "Duke of Warsaw".

On 22 July 1807 Napoleon presented the Duchy with its new constitution, which had been prepared earlier in Dresden. The text was egalitarian in the French style: all men were to be considered equal before the law, and serfdom was abolished. The status of peasants was further clarified by a decree on 21 December 1807:

STANISŁAW MAŁACHOWSKI (1736–1809)

Marshal of the Four Year Seym (1788–92) and member of the "Patriotic Party", he helped shape the Constitution of 3 May. With the creation of the Duchy of Warsaw he became President of the Council of Ministers, and later of the Senate.

DĄBROWSKI ARRIVES IN POZNAŃ

On 6 November 1806, General Jan Henryk Dąbrowski and Józef Wybicki reached Poznań shortly after its liberation by the French army. Huge crowds turned out to greet them, singing the anthem of the Legions "Poland has not yet perished". Dąbrowski immediately called on the citizens of Poznań to rise up against the Prussians in the hope of restoring an independent Poland, and began to raise a Polish army in Wielkopolska. People offered their silver plates and jewellery, and many thousands of volunteers came forward. The high level of Polish patriotism made a lasting impression on Napoleon.

although free from serfdom, the land worked by peasants remained the hereditary property of noblemen. In 1808 the *Code Napoléon* was introduced in Poland; it further underlined noblemen's rights of property ownership. Overall the new laws left the peasants almost as poor and powerless as before.

The Duchy of Warsaw's army was now set to work by Napoleon. A large number of troops were sent to capture the remaining Prussian fortresses including Gdańsk, and about 8,000 men were dispatched to Spain to help in the Peninsular War against Britain and Portugal. There the Polish cavalry, in particular, made their mark in splendid actions such as Somosierra (1808) and Albuhera (1811).

Meanwhile, back in the Duchy of Warsaw a new war began in 1809 when an Austrian army of 32,000 men commanded by Archduke Ferdinand d'Este suddenly marched into the Duchy. General Józef Poniatowski had barely 12,000 troops at his disposal, but decided not to avoid battle. The two armies met at Raszyn near Warsaw on 19 April, and fought an indecisive action. Realizing that he was hopelessly outnumbered, Poniatowski retreated, abandoning Warsaw to the Austrians. Rather than act defensively, he marched on Galicia, and

JÓZEF ZAJĄCZEK (1752–1826)

A general of the Polish army during the war of 1792–93, he become a member of the Highest Council of State during the 1794 Rising, and commanded a Polish division under Napoleon. In 1815 he was appointed Viceroy of the Congress Kingdom, and remained pro-Russian to the end of his political career.

occupied Lublin, Zamość, Sandomierz and Kraków. With their supply lines cut and French forces threatening their rear, the Austrians had to withdraw. Napoleon completed the victory by defeating the Austrians near the Danube at the battles of Wagram and Aspern–Essling. The Duchy of Warsaw benefited greatly from the successes of 1809, and was enlarged to 142,000 square kilometres and 4.3 million inhabitants; Poniatowski's forces were also increased to 60,000 men.

In 1812 the Duchy of Warsaw's army took part in Napoleon's expedition to Moscow. Of the 670,000 men making up the French *Grand Armée*, nearly 100,000 were Poles. On 7 April 1812 the Fifth (Polish) Corps under Poniatowski played a key part in the epic battle of Borodino against the Russians. French and Polish casualties were alarmingly heavy, but the road to Moscow was cleared, and Napoleon marched triumphantly into the Russian capital.

Within days, however, it became obvious that Moscow would be impossible to hold. With the Russian winter falling, Napoleon reluctantly ordered a withdrawal. The retreat from Moscow has entered legend – it was Napoleon's greatest disaster. As the *Grande Armée* trudged through the winter snows of Russia, soldiers froze

CONSTITUTION OF THE DUCHY OF WARSAW

In July 1807 Napoleon presented the Duchy of Warsaw with its Constitution (*as shown in Marcello Bacciarelli's painting*). The document gave the Seym the power to pass laws, and widened the number of persons allowed to vote. A key passage read: "No person either cleric or civilian or judiciary, can govern unless he is a citizen of the Duchy of Warsaw." In reality the King of Saxony (as Duke of Warsaw) had considerable power including the right to pass his own laws.

to death in their thousands, and the Polish contingent lost nearly 70 percent of its strength. Following in the French army's frostbitten footsteps, the Russians entered the Duchy of Warsaw in early 1813.

General Poniatowski managed to partly rebuild the Duchy's forces, and followed Napoleon's retreat into the German states. In November 1813 Napoleon suffered another serious defeat at Leipzig, and Poniatowski, now a marshal of France, was killed in the battle's closing stages. Within months Paris fell to the Allied armies, and Napoleon was sent into exile on the small Mediterranean island of Elba. It is a mark of his esteem for his Polish troops that he took with him among his personal body-guard a single squadron of Polish lancers.

In 1815 Napoleon made a brief attempt to restore his empire, but was defeated at Waterloo. His failure also signalled the end of the Duchy of Warsaw, the fate of which was sealed at the Congress of Vienna in 1815, where the Allied powers decided the future of Europe without the troublesome French emperor.

Napoleon had never granted Poland what the Poles who served him so selflessly had asked – independence. To him the Duchy of Warsaw was merely a useful way of raising troops. He did not even call the country by its proper name. But without any doubt the legend of Napoleon, and the part that Poles had played in build-ing his empire, helped maintain the Polish Question on the international agenda for the next 100 years.

THE BATTLE OF RASZYN

In April 1809 the Austrians invaded the Duchy of Warsaw with 32,000 men. Poniatowski with only 12,000 Duchy troops intercepted them at Raszyn on 19 April – on a site he had chosen earlier because of its favourable terrain. Leading his men forward, he held the Austrians back all day, but was forced to retreat on Warsaw under the cover of darkness. Austrian losses were over 2,500; the Poles lost 450 killed and 900 wounded. Among the dead was the poet Cyprian Godebski (born 1765), a veteran of the Kościuszko Insurrection and the Legions.

PONIATOWSKI AT THE BATTLE OF LEIPZIG

Born in 1763, Prince Józef Poniatowski was the son of the the last king of Poland's brother. His military career began in Austrian service, where friends called him "Pepi". In 1789 he returned to Poland at the urging of his uncle King Stanisław August, and was appointed general of the army.

Józef Poniatowski took part in the 1792–93 war against Russia, distinguishing himself at the battle of Zieleńce. In the Duchy of Warsaw he was appointed Minister for War and supreme commander of the armed forces. During the 1812 campaign he commanded V (Polish) Corps in Napoleon's *Grand Armée*. Poniatowski reached the pinnacle (and end) of his career at the battle of Leipzig, 16–19 October 1813. Known as the "Battle of the Nations", this three-day action saw Napoleon outnumbered by a coalition of Prussians, Austrians, Swedes and Russians. Poniatowski was appointed a Marshal of France and commanded French troops as well as the Polish VIII Corps. On the battle's final day Poniatowski screened the withdrawal of Napoleon's defeated army, and then attempted to retire himself. Unfortunately the only bridge across the River Elster was blown prematurely. Wounded four times, he drowned while attempting to swim the river (as shown in January Suchodolski's painting). His body received a place of honour among the royal tombs at Wawel in Kraków.

THE DUCHY OF WARSAW, 1807–1813

Austrian Partition territory, added to the Duchy in 1809
the Free City of Danzig (Gdańsk), subject to France

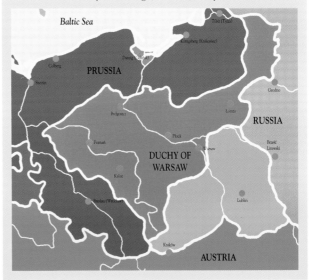

THE RUSSIAN PARTITION

Of the three partitioning powers Russia had the leading position, not merely as the initiator of the Partitions, but also in terms of the amount of land taken – nearly 60% of Poland's territory and half of its population.

The Partitions of Poland were, in large part, the work of the Russian empress Catherine the Great. She had seen Poland as a potential enemy of Russia and had done everything in her power to reduce the threat – first, by attempting to maintain the "Polish anarchy"; and second, by instigating the Partitions. The situation changed after her death in 1796. The new tsar, her son Paul I, was well disposed towards Poland. He admired Kościuszko and authorized his release from a Petersburg jail along with many of his companions.

The Napoleonic wars brought another change in Polish–Russian relations. Napoleon's disastrous expedition to Russia in 1812 saw the shattering of France's power, and the re-occupation of the Duchy of Warsaw by Russian troops. The Duchy's fate was decided in 1815 at the Congress of Vienna. Tsar Alexander I suggested the creation of a new "Kingdom of Poland" on the former territories of the Duchy of Warsaw, which would be under his protection (and control). His idea was approved, though the kingdom never had a Polish king, and is now generally termed the Congress Kingdom* (*Kongresówka*), after the Viennese Congress that set it up.

At first the Congress Kingdom had a territory of 127,000 square kilometres, and 3.3 million inhabitants. Its constitution, which had been written with the help of a Pole, Prince Adam Jerzy Czartoryski, was presented by the tsar on 27 November 1815. The main points were as follows:

- The Congress Kingdom to be linked with Russia through the tsar, who is also king of Poland.
- Personal freedoms and property rights guaranteed.
- Freedom of the press and of worship guaranteed.
- Polish to be the official language of government

Although the terms of the Constitution were far from

WALERIAN ŁUKASIŃSKI (1786–1868)

An infantry major in the Congress Kingdom, he helped set up the National Freemasonry organization, which later became the Patriotic Society. He was arrested in 1822, and spent nearly 40 years in the Schlüsselburg prison in Russia.

THE "NOVEMBER NIGHT"

The night of 29/30 November 1830 saw the chaotic start of the November Rising. It began when a mob led by officers from Warsaw's Infantry Cadet School attempted to steal weapons from military stores. After killing a number of Polish generals who tried to stop the riot, the mob stormed the Warsaw Arsenal (*as shown in Marcin Zaleski's painting*). A second group of civilian conspirators broke into the Belvedere Palace to assassinate the Tsar's brother Grand Duke Constantine, but he escaped.

PIOTR WYSOCKI (1797–1874)

An instructor at the Infantry Cadet School, he was the leader of the plot to seize Warsaw which sparked off the November Rising. During the defence of Warsaw in 1831 he was wounded and captured. He remained in Siberia until a general amnesty was declared in 1857.

* Words marked by an asterisk are explained in the glossary on pages 124–125.

ÓZEF CHŁOPICKI
1771–1854)

A veteran of the Kościuszko
nsurrection and the Legions,
ie fought in Spain and in the
Moscow expedition of 1812,
ising to the rank of general in
he Congress Kingdom.
Appointed "Dictator" for a
period during the November
Rising, he was severely
wounded at the battle of
Grochów on 25 February 1831.

IGNACY PRĄDZYŃSKI
(1792–1850)

A veteran of Napoleon's 1809
and 1812 campaigns, he
became a general and chief of
staff in the November Rising.
Proving to be an excellent
strategist, he was largely
responsible for the victories at
Dębe Wielkie and Iganie. He
also designed the Augustowski
Canal in the Mazurian Lake
District (1824–39).

severe, Russia remained firmly in the driving seat. The
Namiestnik or Viceroy, who represented the tsar in the
Congress Kingdom, was a Pole, Józef Zajączek; but the
supreme commander of the Polish army was the tsar's
brother, Grand Duke Constantine. He used the army as a
plaything, and was widely hated.

It was not long before secret nationalist organizations
began to form in student circles. The most famous was the
Society of Philomaths, founded at Wilno University in
1816 with the poet Adam Mickiewicz among its members. Others included *Panta Koina* (Greek for "Everything
in Common") set up at Warsaw University in 1817, and
the Union of Free Poles which succeeded it in 1820. In
1819 such activities spread to the army when Walerian
Łukasiński helped set up the National Freemasonry organization. Although the ultimate aim of such groups was
liberation, their activities were, at first, mostly peaceful.

Towards the end of 1828 a more radical faction
emerged among young officers at the Infantry Cadet
School in Warsaw. Led by an instructor, Lieutenant Piotr
Wysocki, the group was ready in November 1830 to rise
against Russian rule. On the evening of 29 November the
cadets gained the support of a mob and stormed the
Warsaw Arsenal, capturing weapons. Meanwhile, a group
of civilian co-conspirators attacked the Belvedere Palace
and attempted to kill Grand Duke Constantine. He
escaped, but refused to call out the Russian garrison,
stating adamantly that the revolt was a Polish internal
problem. When, however, Polish troops were mustered,
they refused to fire on the rioters. Amazingly, by midnight
Warsaw was in rebel hands.

With no real political plans, Wysocki handed over
leadership to the civil authorities in Warsaw. Initial talks
were held with Grand Duke Constantine in an attempt to
defuse the situation, but the tsar wanted blood. On 5
December 1830 the Polish authorities gave General Józef
Chłopicki dictatorial powers, but his attempts at a peaceful settlement failed and he was replaced in January 1831.
The Seym became more aggressive, and on 25 January
deposed the Romanov tsars from the Polish throne.
Military actions began in February 1831 when a Russian
army of 115,000 men under Ivan Diebitsch crossed the
border and marched towards Warsaw. The Polish army at
first numbered 50,000, but was better trained and better

JÓZEF DWERNICKI
(1779–1857)

A general in the Congress
Kingdom from 1829, he was
appointed divisional general
after the battle of Stoczek in
February 1831. In the early
spring of 1831 he led a raid
into Volhynia hoping to spread
the rising into the Ukraine;
his small force successfully
diverted a large Russian corps.
He later emigrated to Paris.

JAN SKRZYNECKI
(1787–1860)

Another Napoleonic war
veteran, he became Polish
commander-in-chief during
the November Rising. His
ineffective delaying tactics and
botched peace-making attempts
led eventually to his dismissal.
After the rising he left for
Belgium, where he helped
reorganize the Belgian army,
returning to Poland in 1839.

officered than its Russian adversary: unlike the risings of the 1790s, the November Rising was far from a foregone conclusion. The first major actions took place at Stoczek (14 February) and at Grochów near Warsaw (25 February), and halted the Russian advance. A Polish counter-offensive saw further remarkable victories at Dębe Wielkie (31 March) and Iganie (10 April). Soon the rising had spread to Lithuania.

But the situation changed for the worse as a political crisis developed in Warsaw. The President of the ruling council of the Seym, Prince Adam Jerzy Czartoryski, still hoped for a peaceful settlement with the Russians, but the government splintered as radical elements gained the upper hand. Fearing a full peasant revolution, some Polish landowners even sided with the Russians.

Neither was the army free from discord. When General Chłopicki was badly wounded at the battle of Grochów in February 1831, he was replaced by a more dilatory man, General Jan Skrzynecki. After failing to follow up the Polish successes of the early spring Skrzynecki fell back, allowing Diebitsch to regroup the Russian army. At Ostrołęka on 26 May Skrzynecki suffered a dreadful defeat, losing much of his best infantry. It was the turning point of the war.

The death of Marshal Diebitsch from cholera in June 1831 did not long hinder the Russian advance; his post as commander-in-chief was soon filled by Ivan Pashkievich. By August the government in Warsaw was in chaos. Widespread disgust for Skrzynecki finally brought about his dismissal, but no one could agree on who should replace him. After violent public riots, General Jan Krukowiecki was appointed "Dictator", but he too was replaced when it became apparent that he was talking peace with the Russians. The final act of the rising was the defence of Warsaw: on 8 September, after horrific carnage, Russian troops stormed into the capital, and the Polish government surrendered.

The tsar was determined that such a rebellion could never happen again. Polish officers who had fought in the rising were transported to camps in Russia, while the ordinary soldiers were drafted into Russian regiments. Thousands of landowners who had supported the rising lost their property. More than 10,000 Poles, mainly noblemen, escaped abroad, mostly to France, Belgium and America.

The November Rising was followed by systematic repression: all attempts at independent action by Poles were ruthlessly stamped out. The Russian commander Ivan Pashkievich was made Viceroy of the Congress Kingdom. His reign of terror was marked by the building

○ key battles of the November Rising, 1830–1831

Baltic Sea

KINGDOM OF PRUSSIA

Ostrołęka
Modlin
Grochów
Warsaw · Iganie
Wawer · Stoczek
Dębe Wielkie

RUSSIAN EMPIRE

Kalisz

Dęblin

CONGRESS KINGDOM OF POLAND

Częstochowa

Sandomierz   Zamość

AUSTRIAN EMPIRE

JÓZEF BEM (1784–1850)
An officer in the Duchy of Warsaw's army, he commanded the artillery during the November Rising, and distinguished himself at the battles of Iganie and Ostrołęka and during the defence of Warsaw, escaping abroad after its fall. He became a war hero in Hungary during the revolts known as the "Spring of the Peoples" (1848–49). He died in Syria while in Turkish service.

JAN KRUKOWIECKI (1769–1850)

Educated in Vienna, he joined the Duchy of Warsaw's army in 1806, rising to general by the time of the November Rising. He was appointed president of the National Government in 1831, and "dictator" in the rising's final stages. After years of penal servitude in the depths of Russia, he was allowed to return to Poland.

BATTLE OF IGANIE

On 10 April 1831, 7,000 Poles under General Ignacy Prądzyński defeated 11,000 Russian troops at Iganie. But the indecisive Polish commander-in-chief, Jan Skrzynecki, failed to follow up the victory.

THE DEFENCE OF WARSAW

In March 1831, with a Russian attack imminent, the men and women of Warsaw came out to repair the city's fortifications. Despite their efforts, Warsaw's earthworks were penetrated in fierce Russian assaults in September, and the rising collapsed.

BATTLE OF OSTROŁĘKA

The decisive action of the November Rising took place on 26 May 1831. Skrzynecki deployed in small bodies rather than organizing mass attacks. He lost 6,500 men, but escaped thanks to an artillery screen set up by Józef Bem, which halted the victorious Russians.

of the Warsaw Citadel, a fortress north of the Old Town, where political prisoners were held and executed.

In emigrant circles, the reasons for the failure of the November Rising were analysed in detail, as were the methods by which the struggle for independence should proceed. From his headquarters in the Hotel Lambert in Paris, Prince Czartoryski gathered around him a group of aristocrats who believed in armed insurrection with the support of England and France. A rival organization, the Polish Democratic Society, also in France, believed that independence would come only with the support of the workers of other European countries. But it was not until the 1860s, a generation later, that another serious attempt at seizing independence was made.

The revolt which came to be known as the January Rising was caused in large part by the overzealous sup-

pression of demonstrations commemorating the thirtieth anniversary of the 1831 Insurrection. In April 1861 many civilians were killed in Warsaw's Castle Square when the Russian authorities broke up a public protest. More killings followed and a state of emergency was declared. By the winter of 1861/62 the Warsaw Citadel was crammed with thousands of political prisoners; but such brutalities simply increased the troubles they were intended to quell.

A radical "Red" party began to emerge, with armed revolt as its main goal. It included intellectuals, artisans, students, and even serving Polish officers in the Russian army. Aware that a revolt was being planned, the tsar authorized the Polish Margrave Alexander Wielopolski (1803–77), representing the moderate "White" party, to take drastic action. Wielopolski had 100,000 Russian troops brought into the Congress Kingdom, hoping to remove potential troublemakers in a single stroke by conscripting all young men into the Russian army. Forewarned of the "Branka" or forced conscription scheduled to take place on 14 January 1863, thousands of Poles slipped off into the forest.

One week later, on the night of 22/23 January 1863, the January Rising began. A new National Government was set up, and called on Poles to fight for their motherland. From the start the rising took on the character of a guerrilla war. More than 1,000 military actions were won or lost. Even the largest – at Węgrów, Małogoszcz, Miechów and Siemiatycze – were mere skirmishes.

THE GREAT EMIGRATION

After the collapse of the November Rising, Poles escaped to Britain, Belgium, Switzerland, Germany, the US, and above all to France. The French welcomed Polish refugees with open arms (*as in this lithograph by C. Malankiewicz*). Polish immigrants were even given a monthly allowance to support themselves. Paris quickly became the centre of Polish cultural life abroad.

ADAM JERZY CZARTORYSKI (1770–1861)

Polish magnate and politician, regarded by many as the "uncrowned king of Poland". After taking part in the 1792–93 war against Russia, he went to St Petersburg and was befriended by the future Tsar Alexander I. In 1804 he was appointed Russia's minister of foreign affairs, and from 1813 became personal advisor to the tsar, a relationship that ended in 1815. During the November Rising of 1831 he was President of the National Government, and later escaped to Paris, where he set up a political group based at the Hotel Lambert.

THE "BRANKA"

Military service in the Russian empire lasted 30 years. Few men volunteered willingly, as the chances of returning home again were remote. The Russian answer was the *Branka* – forced conscription, carried out in the middle of the night. Young recruits were chosen by lottery (as in Artur Grottger's picture, *above*) and were then escorted under armed guard to their future regiments (*below*). The *Branka* of 14 January 1863 was ordered by the Russian authorities to remove potential Polish troublemakers, and was the direct cause of the January Rising of 1863–64.

ROMUALD TRAUGUTT (1826–1864)

"Dictator" of Poland in the final stages of the January Rising. He had served as an officer in the Russian army from 1845 to 1862. Working secretly from a Warsaw house under the nose of the Russians, he helped reorganize Polish forces, and tried to raise new peasant troops. His arrest on 11 April 1864 and execution on 5 August ended the January Rising.

compared with the battles of the November Rising. But a charismatic leader to stir the nation was lacking. Infighting paralysed the command structure, and the leadership of the rising changed with baffling regularity.

Finally, in October 1863, Romuald Traugutt was given dictatorial powers in a last ditch attempt to save the rising. His arrest in April 1864, and subsequent execution by hanging at the Warsaw Citadel, brought the insurrection to a close. The rebel's cause had, in fact, already been dealt its fatal blow by an edict from the tsar in March 1864. By giving the Polish peasants land he took away their main grievance, and removed them as a source of manpower for the insurrectionists.

The aftermath of the January Rising was repression even more severe than after the 1831 rising. Thousands were deported to camps in Siberia. The Polish flavour of the Congress Kingdom was systematically eradicated, and Russian replaced Polish as the language of government and schooling. Even Poland's name was abolished – it became merely "Vistula Land" (*Pryvislinskiy Kray*).

By the 1870s the Polish independence movement in Russia became linked with the Europe-wide interest in communism, and led to the creation of leftist political parties. The Proletariat Party was founded in 1882 by Ludwik Waryński; when its leaders were arrested, remnants transferred to the Polish Socialist Party (PPS) formed in 1892. Among its members was a certain Józef Piłsudski, editor of PPS's illegal newspaper *The Worker*. Another major new party was Social Democracy of the Kingdom of Poland (later "of Poland and Lithuania"), which believed in the international unity of all workers. In truth it was to have less influence in Polish affairs than in the political storm developing in Russia. Its leaders included two Poles who became internationally famous: Rosa Luxemburg (founder of the communist movement in Germany), and Felix Dzierżynski ("father" of the Bolshevik secret police, the *Cheka*).

The year 1905 saw widespread strikes across the Russian empire, resulting in the first Russian revolution. Poles played an active role, and even managed to have the Polish language reintroduced in government offices and many schools. But it became clear that from the Polish province of the Russian empire there was no visible path to independent statehood.

THE PRUSSIAN PARTITION

Prussia took part in all three of the Partitions, annexing 20 percent of Poland's land along with 2.7 million inhabitants. It is often said that "Prussian Poles" accepted assimilation into the German Reich with little resistance; in reality their struggle for independence was to be as active as in the other Partitions.

Napoleon played an important part in the history of the Prussian Partition. In October 1806, after destroying the Prussian army in the twin battles of Jena and Auerstedt, he marched onto Polish soil. His arrival set off a popular rising against Prussian rule in Wielkopolska. The lands of the Prussian Partition were to form the greater part of the Duchy of Warsaw, which Napoleon established in 1807. France's eventual defeat led to the collapse of the Duchy. In its place the 1815 Congress of Vienna created the Grand Duchy of Posen (Poznań), again mostly out of previously Prussian lands.

The Duchy of Posen had an area of 29,000 square kilometres and a population of 776,000. Its first Grand Duke was Friedrich Wilhelm III (1770–1840), who had been the king of Prussia since 1797. He believed in the equality of the Duchy's Polish and German inhabitants and approved the use of the Polish language in schools, lawcourts and government. His viceroy was Prince Anton Radziwiłł, who married a Prussian duchess.

The Prussian army had successfully prevented the November Rising of 1831 from spreading into Posnania* though the "Prussian Poles" and Germans were openly sympathetic to the plight of the "Russian Poles". After the failure of the rising, many Polish military units escaped from the Congress Kingdom and were welcomed openly in Posnania. But the freedoms that "Prussian Poles" had enjoyed were slowly reduced. The Polish viceroy was replaced by a German president, Edward Flotwell. Many Polish landowners were stripped of their estates, which were handed over to Prussians. The Polish language became frowned on, and from 1832 German became the official language of government.

HIPOLIT CEGIELSKI (1815–1868)

Originally a Poznań schoolteacher, he was dismissed for refusing to conduct searches in the houses of his students after the Kraków Revolution. In 1846 he opened a shop in Poznań's Hotel Bazaar; it was so successful that he became a major industrialist, and set up a factory producing tools and farm machinery, which still bears his name today. He also published the newspaper *Gazeta Polska*, which later became the *Dziennik Poznański*.

KAROL MARCINKOWSKI (1800–1846)

Born in Poznań, he worked originally as a doctor and played an active part in the November Rising. In 1833 he received a gold medal from the French Academy of Sciences for a treatise on the great killer of the 19th century, cholera. He was largely responsible for the building of Poznań's Hotel Bazar. In 1841 he set up the Society for Educational Assistance which gave scholarships to poor students.

HOTEL BAZAR

Built between 1838 and 1841, Poznań's Hotel Bazar included shops, meeting rooms, as well as modern hotel facilities. It soon became a gathering place for intellectuals, noblemen and townsfolk, and the centre of Polish cultural and economic life in the Prussian Partition.

The defeat of the November Rising caused the richer echelons of society to abandon any ideas of a direct revolt. Instead they turned to what they considered a more pressing task: the raising of the economic and cultural levels of what was still a backward country. A typical representative of the new views was Karol Marcinkowski. A doctor who had taken active part in the November Rising, and mixed with the Hotel Lambert group in Paris, he returned to his birthplace Poznań to put into reality the ideas of a more constructive way of resisting Prussian domination. He was largely responsible for the building, between 1838 and 1841, of the Hotel Bazar in Poznań which became an important Polish cultural centre. In 1841 he helped found the Society for Educational Assistance which awarded scholarships to poor students.

Dr Marcinkowski was not alone; other enterprising Poles were concentrated especially in the Poznań area. They included Gustaw Potworowski, who set up the Gostyń "casino" (then a hall for public meetings and social functions rather than a gambling house). It was a valuable addition to the local cultural facilities.

In 1848 the revolutionary movement known as the "Spring of the Peoples" swept through Europe, and into the Polish lands. The leader of the largest rising in the Duchy of Posen was Ludwik Mierosławski, who had earlier been condemned to death after attempting to start an insurrection in 1846. In March 1848, during revolutionary disturbances in Germany, Mierosławski was released from his Berlin prison. His arrival in Poznań stirred the Polish population to action. Prussian officials were forced from their posts, and a Polish militia was organized. Stalling for time, the Prussians promised the Duchy self-rule. When they changed their mind, an armed rising broke out.

The Polish rebel forces lost a battle at Książ, but won victories at Miłosław and at Sokołowo near Września. When the Prussians sent in more troops many Polish officers ceased to believe that the war could be won, and began to leave the ranks. On 9 May Mierosławski resigned as leader, and an act of capitulation was signed shortly after. Like all failed Polish attempts at independence in the 19th century, the 1848 revolt brought punishment. The Grand Duchy of Posen was demoted in stature, becoming merely Provinz-Posen.

With the failure of the 1848 rising and the equally unsuccessful 1863 January Rising, the "Prussian Poles" switched even more decidedly away from ideas of revolt towards the constructive approach pioneered by Dr Marcinkowski. The future was seen to lie in economic progress. Poland had no hope of reaching independence unless she could compete on cultural and economic terms with her neighbours. Such activities began to be known as "organic work", so called because society could be seen

LUDWIK MIEROSŁAWSKI (1814–1878)

Born in France, he took part in the November Rising of 1830–31. After revolutionary activity in 1846 he was sentenced to death in Berlin, but was set free in March 1848, and became leader of the Poznań Rising. He suffered further defeats during risings in Sicily (1849) and Baden (1849). In 1863 he was appointed "Dictator" of the January Rising, but never took command. Afterwards he left for Paris, where he remained until his death.

BATTLE OF MIŁOSŁAW

On 30 April 1848 Polish forces commanded by General Ludwik Mierosławski met a Prussian army under General Blumen at Miłosław. Despite being outnumbered almost two-to-one, Mierosławski's forces gained the upper hand and won a minor victory.

as a living organism which needed careful nurturing. Also influential was the latest French philosophy of "positivism" – which recognized only knowledge based on concrete facts and observations. The romantic idealism connected with the fight for freedom was set aside for the long-term benefits of hard work, and faith in the progress of science.

The new spirit of enterprise saw the creation of Poland's first Agricultural Society in Piaseczno, which (along with new workers' cooperatives in the towns) began to grant loans. In 1871 the Union of Agricultural Cooperatives was formed with a priest, Piotr Wawrzyniak, at its head. Another progressive organization was the Society for Educational Assistance, directed for many years by the entrepreneur Hipolit Cegielski. In 1872 Poznań saw the beginnings of the Society for Popular Learning, which aimed to open Polish libraries in backward rural areas. The Prussian authorities soon closed it down, only for it to re-emerge in 1880 as the Society of People's Libraries.

Despite increasing prosperity, the status of Poles in the Prussian Partition became difficult, especially after 1867, when Posnania became part of the North German Union, and more so in 1871, when Germany was united under Prussian leadership. Under the Chancellor of the new German Reich, Otto von Bismarck, the Polish lands became the target of intensive Germanization. In this new *Kulturkampf*, or "war of cultures", efforts were directed against all Polish institutions. Between 1872 and 1874 the Polish language was virtually eliminated from the school system as native Polish teachers were replaced by Germans, and in 1876 its use was banned in the lawcourts and government. From 1887 the study of Polish in schools, even as a second language, was forbidden. The final bastion of Polishness was the Catholic Church, and here the Prussian authorities made special efforts to reduce its influence. A law in 1873 made the Church officially dependent on the state. When the Archbishop of Poznań and Gniezno, Mieczysław Ledóchowski, complained about state interference and protested at the harassing of Polish clergymen, he was arrested and received a two-year prison sentence.

Germanization gathered pace. In 1886 Chancellor Bismarck created the Colonization Commission to encourage German settlers. From its copious funds it se

OTTO VON BISMARCK
(1815–1898)

One of Poland's most dogged enemies, and the creator of *Kulturkampf* – the "struggle between cultures". He became premier of the Prussian government in 1861, and in 1871, after the unification of Germany, was made chancellor of the German Reich.

PIOTR
WAWRZYNIAK
(1849–1910)

Born at Wyrzyce near Śrem, he was of peasant origin. After studying at seminaries in Poznań and Gniezno he was ordained as a priest in 1872. In the new spirit of "organic progress" his interests soon stretched far beyond the spiritual welfare of his parishioners.

He helped organize the Bank Ludowy (People's Bank) in Śrem, became patron of the Union of Agricultural Cooperatives, and served as an envoy to the Prussian assembly in Berlin. From 1904 he was director of the St Wojciech printing-house and bookshop in Poznań, which still exists today (*photo right*).

about purchasing land from Poles for sale at a discount to Germans. Polish landowners fought back with the creation of a Land Bank, with some success.

Even more insidious was the *Deutscher Ostmarken-verein* (German Society for the Eastern Borders) founded in 1894. Popularly known as the *Hakata* – from the first name of its founders, Hansemann, Kennemann and Tiedemann – its aim was to promote German culture at the expense of the Slavic, which according to the latest German "scientific" theories was racially inferior. Staffed by Prussians, the *Hakata* had support in the highest places, not least from the German Reich's new chancellor, Prince Bernhard von Bülow.

The Prussian authorities issued laws aimed to prevent Poles from building new farms, and even from speaking in Polish at public meetings. Resistance to the systematic destruction of Polish culture was almost futile, the most famous incident being the schoolchildren's strike at Września in 1901, provoked by the banning of the Polish language in religious studies.

The Polish spirit refused to be beaten, as the celebrated case of Michał Drzymała was to show. In 1904 the Prussian authorities refused to grant him permission to build a house on his own land. He moved into a gypsy caravan, but the authorities had it removed on the grounds of "safety". Undeterred, and with the help of public contributions

he was soon able to purchase a new caravan. Only after a protracted five-year legal battle did the Prussian authorities again manage to evict the Poznanian patriot. The case was widely reported, and even reached the international press. Drzymała's lone stand against the full weight of Prussian bureaucracy became a symbol of the fight against Germanization.

DRZYMAŁA'S CARAVAN

The son of a peasant, Michał Drzymała (1857–1937) became famous for his long dispute with the Prussian authorities. He later recounted the story:
"A plague on these Krauts, who refused to give me permission to build a house …
I learned of a barkeeper, Kideman, who had a circus caravan in his yard.… Well, within a week it was mine.… People came to look at the caravan, and I, after a time, was charged with organizing illegal gatherings and was sent to jail."
In 1939 the village in which his caravan stood was renamed Drzymałowo in honour of this unlikely Polish hero.

THE WRZEŚNIA SCHOOLCHILDREN'S STRIKE

In 1901, in the school at Września in Wielkopolska, the children protested at the banning of the Polish language from religious studies, the last subject in which its use had been permitted.
After refusing to reply to questions in German, the children were caned. Their parents immediately complained, provoking a sadistic reaction from the Prussian authorities. Several parents were imprisoned for spells of two years.
A museum of the strike can be visited in Września today.

THE AUSTRIAN PARTITION

Austria took part in only two of Poland's partitions – in 1772 and 1795. In all the Austrian Partition included 20 percent of Poland's territory and 3.8 million people. It was known officially as the Kingdom of Galicia and Lodomeria, or simply "Galicia".

After Austria's humiliating defeat in the War of 1809 (see page 69), large areas of the Austrian Partition became part of the Duchy of Warsaw. These territories were recovered by Austria after the Congress of Vienna in 1815, with the exception of Kraków which was set up as a Free City. With a population of 88,000 and an area of 1,164 square kilometres, the so-called Kraków Republic was to be overseen by all three of the Partitioning Powers.

Because of its unique status and geographical position, Kraków became a centre for the Polish independence movement. It was the last refuge for rebel troops during the November Rising of 1831, and became a way-station for persons escaping to France. The Russians, in particular, were determined that the Free City should be closed down. The pretext finally came with the so-called Kraków Revolution of 1846.

The insurrection, which lasted only nine days, was something of a disaster from the beginning. The original plan had been for the revolt to start simultaneously in all the Partitions, but only days before the planned outbreak many key leaders including Ludwik Mierosławski were arrested (see page 79). Only in Kraków did the rising go ahead on any scale. Even there events were hampered by a hostile peasant revolt led by Jakub Szela, who saw the Polish noblemen rather than the Austrian authorities as his main enemy. Within days the Kraków Revolution had splintered into rival political factions. When troops of the three Partitioning Powers arrived the revolt collapsed completely. Punishment was swift. The Kraków Republic was dissolved and its territories were incorporated into Galicia.

The next disturbance was not long in coming. When the popular revolts known as the "Spring of the Peoples" broke out throughout Europe in 1848, the ailing Austrian Empire was one of the most disrupted states. The barricades went up again in Kraków, and – with more determination – in the Galician capital Lwów (then Lemberg). But the revolt never took on the scale that it did elsewhere in the Austrian lands. The most significant event took place on 22 April 1848, when the governor of Galicia, Count Franz von Stadion, abolished the hated peasant labour dues (pańszczyzna*). The peasants received their own land and serfdom was ended at long last.

At the end of 1860s, with the Austrian Empire growing ever weaker, the Poles of Galicia achieved an increasing decree of autonomy. A Polish seym and council were set up, and Polish again became the official language of schooling and administration. Poles were permitted to hold government posts and to send representatives to the Reichsrat in Vienna; on several occasions Poles rose to the highest posts in the Austrian government, even reaching the premiership of the Vienna cabinet.

Polish political organizations blossomed in Galicia and many were to survive well into the 20th century. A Peasant Party emerged in 1895, changing its name in 1903 to the Polish Peasant Party (Polskie Stronnictwo Ludowe - PSL). It sought mainly to empower the poor farmers of Galicia, who still had an uphill struggle against the great

Republic of Kraków

* Words marked by an asterisk are explained in the glossary on pages 124–125.

"We will win for our-selves a structure of society in which every person will be able to make use of the fruits of the land according to his merits and his talents, in which there will be no place for privilege in any form...."

THE KRAKÓW REVOLUTION

On 22 February 1846 Polish insurgents freed Kraków of Austrian control, and announced the creation of a new "National Government". On the same day they published *Manifesto for the Polish Nation* (*above*) which promised wide-ranging reforms of Polish society. The privileges of the higher social classes were to be abolished, peasants were be relieved of labour dues and to receive their own land. The proposals were well received in Kraków, but within days the new leaders began to disagree among themselves. By 4 March the Kraków Revolution had collapsed.

DEMBOWSKI'S PROCESSION

On 27 February 1846 a religious procession marched to Podgórze, a suburb of Kraków marking the Austrian border. At its head was one of the leaders of the Kraków Revolution, the 24-year-old Edward Dembowski. The procession's chief goal was to dissuade the peasants from co-operating with the Austrian army against the Revolution. Austrian troops, believing they were facing hostile insurgents, opened fire on the peaceful column and Dembowski, cross in hand, was killed.

estates run by nobles. The PSL also fought for reform in the electoral system and for wider access to education. The year 1897 saw the formation of the National Democracy Party – known popularly, from its initials as *Endecja*. Its main objective was Polish independence. Under its leader Roman Dmowski, Endecja soon became the most important party in Poland.

Although the Austrian Partition remained economically the most backward of the former Polish territories, it had freedoms of which Poles in the Russian and Prussian Partitions could only dream. Polish culture was allowed to develop without interference from the central authorities, as we shall see in the next chapter.

The Kościuszko Mound towers above fortifications built by the Austrians outside Kraków.

JAKUB SZELA

A peasant from the village of Smarzowa in the Tarnów district, Jakub Szela was the main leader of violent peasant disturbances that struck Galicia at the time of the Kraków Revolution. Szela's peasants burned hundreds of Polish estates and killed over 1,000 noblemen. In reward for his "services" the Austrian government awarded Szela a large farm.

ECONOMY AND CULTURE IN THE 19TH CENTURY

Despite oppression by the Partitioning Powers, everyday life went on. The Industrial and Agrarian revolutions slowly transformed Poland's towns and countryside; meanwhile dreams of independence were kept alive in the art and literature of Romanticism.

The first decades of the 19th century saw the arrival of the Industrial Revolution in Poland, based on two main products: textiles and coal. The heart of the textile industry was Łódź, which by the end of the century had grown into the third largest cloth producing centre in the world, after Manchester and Lille. The coal mining industry was centred in the Dąbrowa Basin in Upper Silesia, on one of the world's richest coal seams.

An economic boom began in 1851 when customs barriers between the Congress Kingdom and the Russian empire were abolished. By the 1890s nearly 50 percent of Poland's manufactured goods were being exported to Russia. The need for factory labour brought about the rapid growth of towns and also created a demand for mass transportation. The first steam trains appeared in Poland in the mid-1840s, on new railroads that linked the main industrial centres. The first electric trams appeared in Bydgoszcz in 1888. Gas streetlamps were also installed in the fashionable areas of many Polish city centres.

Despite industrialization, the greater part of the Polish lands remained poor and rural in character. The Agrarian revolution had its greatest impact in the Prussian Partition thanks to entrepreneurs such as Dezydery Chłapowski, who did much to popularize new western European farming methods. The old three-field system was abandoned in favour of crop rotation, and new machines for reaping and haymaking were introduced along with artificial fertilizers. Knowledge of such techniques was spread through agricultural clubs. At the same time new "land banks", such as the *Bank Ziemski w Poznaniu* formed in 1888, gave financial backing to farmers. The overall result was a considerable increase in the size of harvests.

REVOLUTIONARY MONEY

During the November Rising of 1830–31 the National Government authorized new coins, like this 2-złoty piece. They bore the Polish eagle and Lithuanian knight in place of the hated Tsarist eagle.

DEZYDERY CHŁAPOWSKI (1788–1879)

Born in Turew or Śmigiel, he studied at the military academy in Berlin, and served alongside Jan Henryk Dąbrowski and Napoleon himself, before returning home in search of a more peaceful life in 1813. Dismayed by the backwardness of Polish agriculture, he decided to set up a model farm based on the latest western farming practices, and travelled to England to gain practical experience.

He later wrote down the new techniques in an influential manual entitled simply "On farming".

In the 19th century the steam train replaced the horse-drawn mail coach. The first route on Polish territory was the Warsaw–Vienna Railway, built between 1845 and 1848.

MAKSYMILIAN JACKOWSKI (1815–1905)

The founder of several agricultural clubs which helped introduce the latest western farming methods and made education more available to ordinary people. Such groups also opposed the Germanization of Polish territory. From 1873 he directed the Central Agricultural Society in Wielkopolska.

SEAT OF POLISH LEARNING

The only part of the former Polish lands where Polish culture was allowed to develop freely was the Austrian Partition. The Jagiellonian University in Kraków (of which the Collegium Novum is shown below) became a centre of Polish learning. It attracted students from the Russian and Prussian Partitions, who came to attend lectures by Polish professors in the Polish language.

Galicia, by far the poorest of the former Polish territories, largely missed out on the advances of the Industrial and Agrarian revolutions. On the other hand, the Austrian emperor allowed his Polish subjects civil liberties and a high degree of autonomy. Spurred on by progressive magnates such as Ignacy Potocki and Adam Kazimierz Czartoryski, Galicia saw great advances in Polish culture. The historic Jagiellonian University in Kraków was allowed to retain its Polish identity. Several new institutions were founded, notably the excellent grammar school at Krzemieniec in Volhynia (set up in 1804 by Tadeusz Czacki, with the help of Hugo Kołłątaj) and the Mining School in Kielce (founded in 1816 by Stanisław Staszic). One of Poland's most prestigious academic institutions, the Ossolineum, was founded in Lwów in 1827.

Academic institutions also blossomed in the Russian Partition, though they were susceptible to the whims of the tsar. A law school was set up in Warsaw in 1808, and one year later a medical school. Universities were opened in Wilno (1803) and Warsaw (1816). The latter was closed by the Russian authorities in 1831, although it reopened in 1863 as Warsaw's "Main School" and, in 1869, was renamed the "Tsarist University".

It was in the humanities and arts that the new Polish institutions especially excelled. The 1820s saw the birth of a European cultural movement which had a strong impact on the Polish arts – Romanticism. It was characterized by the love of fantasy and folk themes, with the stress on feelings and emotions rather than the cold facts. Romanticism was especially appealing to the dreamy Polish temperament. Three great Polish Romantic poets emerged, working from Paris: Adam Mickiewicz, Juliusz Słowacki and Zygmunt Krasiński. Back in Poland Aleksander Fredro wrote his famous comedies. Polish music also had its virtuosos: Fryderyk Chopin and Stanisław Moniuszko.

After the collapse of the January Rising in 1864 a more sombre mood prevailed. A fashion for dark clothes and black jewellery was a reflection of a country in mourning. Many Poles set aside their nostalgic idealism, and put their faith in the power of science and money. The watchwords of the new era were positivism, "organic work", philanthropy and, most important of all,

THE THREE PROPHETS OF POLAND

The Romantic movement had its heyday in Poland between 1822 and 1864. It was a trend that despised logic in favour of intuition and imagination. Its influence was felt throughout Polish culture, and was especially strong in literature. Three poets were the undisputed greats of Polish Romanticism:

Adam Mickiewicz, Juliusz Słowacki and Zygmunt Krasiński; they became known as the "Three Prophets" of Poland. A fourth poet, Cyprian Kamil Norwid (1821–83), is often added to this group, but he never received the same degree of acclaim during his lifetime and died in poverty. All four poets worked mainly abroad.

ADAM MICKIEWICZ (1798–1855)

His historical novel *Pan Tadeusz* is regarded as Poland's national epic. Born in Lithuania, he was exiled to Russia for revolutionary agitation, and on release emigrated to Paris. He died in Istanbul while raising Polish troops to fight Russia in the Crimean War.

JULIUSZ SŁOWACKI (1809–1849)

Author of dramatic plays and poetic novels including *Kordian*, *Balladyna* and *Lilla Weneda*. Born in Volhynia, he graduated from Wilno University, and then moved to Warsaw. During the November Rising he escaped to Paris, where he wrote most of his work.

ZYGMUNT KRASIŃSKI (1812–1859)

Born in Paris, he studied in Warsaw and Switzerland. His best known works are *Nie-Boska komedia* (The Undivine Comedy) and *Irydion*. In his letters to Delfina Potocka he left an interesting picture of the Romantic age.

progress. It was believed that hard work would best serve the cause of Polish independence.

The new mood spread into the arts, which now favoured realism and the down-to-earth. In literature the subject of human relationships was tackled by some of Poland's greatest authors: Henryk Sienkiewicz, Bolesław Prus and Eliza Orzeszkowa. The theatres – one of the few public places where the Polish language was permitted – were full, and actors like Helena Modrzejewska and Ludwik Solski became household names. The visual arts thrived, producing painters such as Juliusz Kossak, Jan Matejko and Aleksander Gierymski, who painted in the realistic style fashionable in this period.

The solemn mood which had engulfed Poland in the 1860s was swept aside in the 1890s by a rush of creative talent known as the "Young Poland" movement. This led the way towards a less rigid style of art and has been

THE TEMPLE OF SIBYL

The past was the main influence on the architectural tastes of the 19th century. The Romantic movement was, above all, fascinated by the medieval and ancient worlds, and saw the heyday of the "Neo-Gothic" and "Neo-Classical" styles. Examples of buildings in both styles can be seen in the park and palace complex at Puławy, near Lublin, then the property of the wealthy Czartoryski family. Between 1798 and 1806 Princess Izabela Czartoryska had the park landscaped, giving it many quiet corners, ideal for romantic contemplation. One of the many impressive buildings she commissioned was the neo-classical Temple of Sibyl (*above*), the site of Poland's earliest museum opened in 1801. In it Izabela Czartoryska collected works of art and historical relics of great Poles. The temple, named after a prophetess of Ancient Greece, is also thought to have been a secret meeting place of Polish freemasons.

**MARIA
SKŁODOWSKA-CURIE**

*"I believe that the substance
we have separated from pitch-
blende is a metal that is not
yet known, similar in its
chemical properties to bismuth.
If the existence of this metal is
confirmed, I propose to call it
'polonium' – after the name
of the homeland of one of us."*

It was in these words, in
July 1898, that Maria
Curie modestly described
the discovery she had
made with her husband
Pierre. She shared the
1903 Physics Nobel Prize
with him and with Henri
Becquerel, and in 1911
won the Chemistry Nobel
Prize. Born in Warsaw in
1867, she spent most of
her life in Paris, and died
in 1934 from leukaemia
brought on by her
radiation experiments.

SECESSION

The end of the 19th century saw
a new art style arrive from
Vienna – Secession. Related to
Art Nouveau, it was characterized by wavy lines and pastel
colours. The Society of Fine
Arts building in Kraków (*right*)
was designed in Secession style
by Franciszek Mączyński. The
stained-glass window (*far right*)
was made by the Secession artist
Stanisław Wyspiański.

called a "neo-Romantic" movement. The new optimistic
trend blended the new Western styles – modernism,
impressionism and the Secession – and was to dominate
the arts until World War I. Its exponents included
Poland's greatest playwright Stanisław Wyspiański,
Stefan Żeromski the greatest writer, and Jan Kasprowicz
the greatest poet. Poland's musicians became world
famous, especially the pianist Ignacy Jan Paderewski and
the composer Karol Szymanowski.

The final decades of the 19th century saw a series of
important scientific discoveries by Poles. In 1883
Zygmunt Wróblewski and Karol Olszewski liquefied
oxygen and nitrogen for the first time. In 1898 Maria
Skłodowska-Curie identified two new chemical elements, radium and polonium. She won two Nobel prizes
and became the first woman professor at the Sorbonne in
Paris. Meanwhile in far-off South America Ernest
Malinowski achieved the near impossible when he built
a railroad across the Andes mountains.

**JAN MATEJKO
(1838–1893)**

Poland's greatest historical
painter. A Czech by birth,
after moving to Kraków he
adopted Poland as his
home. Speaking to students
at the School of Fine Arts
in Kraków, he stressed the
political value of his work:
*"Art is at present a sort of
weapon for us, to separate art
from the love of one's country
is simply not allowed."*
Matejko's paintings have
become national treasures,
and many of them, along
with portraits from his
"Gallery of Kings", appear
on the pages of this book.

POLAND AND WORLD WAR I

In 1914 Europe tottered on the brink of the most brutal war yet known; millions would die in the desperate struggle ahead. Yet the human catastrophe brought with it new hope for the rebirth of an independent Poland.

SUPREME NATIONAL COMMITTEE (NKN)

Formed on 16 August 1914 in Kraków, the NKN was tasked with co-ordinating the raising of Polish troops for the Austrian army. One key member was Władysław Sikorski (*seated at centre*), a future premier of Poland.

Europe at the turn of the 20th century was divided into two camps, cemented by alliances. On the strength of the so-called "Triple Entente" Russia was allied with France and Britain. Against them stood the "Central Powers" – the empires of Germany and Austria–Hungary. Poles dreaming of independence had to decide which of the two camps to support.

The pro-Russian faction was represented by the National Democracy Party (known as *Endecja*) with Roman Dmowski at its head. The second faction was, strictly speaking, anti-Russian rather than pro-Austrian or pro-German. It was led by the charismatic figure of Józef Piłsudski, leader of the Polish Socialist Party (PPS). He was convinced that Russia would always be Poland's greatest enemy and was willing to side with the Central Powers if this would help Poland throw off the Russian yoke. Needless to say, the pro- and anti-Russian camps were directly opposed to each other.

Piłsudski had a long history of anti-Russian activity. As early as 1904 he had overseen the formation of a military wing to the PPS, whose *bojówki* or battle squads terrorized tsarist officers and tax collectors, and robbed mailtrains. In 1908 the *bojówki* were replaced by a fledgling Polish army, known as the Union for Active Struggle. At the same time para-military "sporting clubs" sprang up throughout Galicia, followed by a Rifleman's Union. By June 1914 Piłsudski had over 10,000 trained fighting men ready to take up arms against Russia.

Dmowski, meanwhile, believed in gaining greater influence in the Russian empire by legal means. In the first elections to the *Duma* or Russian parliament in 1906, Dmowski's National Democrats had gained 34 seats. As the European crisis deepened this Polish lobby pressed for greater freedoms in the "Vistula Land" province.

At the moment when World War I broke out – with Austria's declaration of war on Serbia on 28 July 1914 – the Partitioning Powers regarded Polish nationalism a[s] irrelevant, and treated the Poles merely as a convenien[t] source of manpower for their armies. Polish committee[s] were set in place to expedite the raising of troops for th[e] war effort. On 27 August Austria officially sanctioned th[e]

ROMAN DMOWSKI (1864–1939)

One of the key figures in 20th-century Polish politics. A co-founder of the National Democracy Party (*Endecja*), he was a political opponent of Piłsudski. During World War I he led the Polish National Committee in France, and headed the Polish delegation at the 1919 Paris Peace Conference.

formation of two Polish Legions under Piłsudski, who were to fight in their own uniforms alongside the Austrians. Meanwhile the Russians allowed Dmowski to begin raising the Puławski Legion, which was to fight at the side of Russia as a rival to Piłsudski's legions.

The attitude of the great powers towards the Polish Question began to change as war casualties mounted. The new military technologies – machine guns, poison gas and massed heavy artillery – reaped a terrible harvest, taking a far heavier toll of human lives than had been expected. By late 1916 the Germans and Austrians had succeeded in capturing most of Russia's Polish territories, but were running short of the manpower they needed to continue the war.

On 5 November 1916 the emperors of Germany and Austria-Hungary, hoping to gain the support of their Polish subjects, announced the creation of a new Polish state, "wrested from Polish territories ruled by Russia".

PIŁSUDSKI'S LEGIONS

The Polish legions – named in imitation of Dąbrowski's legions of a century earlier – were commanded by Józef Piłsudski, and fought from 1914 to 1917 on the side of the Austrians against the Russians. They wore Polish uniforms and were commanded by Austrian officers of Polish origin. They won fame in battles on the Eastern Front, from Laski near Dęblin to the Stochód Valley in Polesie, and were an important symbol of Poland's revival as a military power.

THE CHARGE AT ROKITNA

One of the greatest successes of Piłsudski's legions in World War I was the cavalry charge at Rokitna in June 1915. With great bravado Piłsudski's uhlans successfully carried an assault to the Russian trenches. (Painting by Wojciech Kossak.)

"DECLARATION OF TWO EMPERORS"

On 5 November 1916, in the Chamber of Columns in the Royal Castle at Warsaw, the German General-Governor Hans von Beseler read out an act which created a Polish state supervised by the Emperors of Austria and Germany. The country was to be controlled by a Provisional Council of State, with Józef Piłsudski in charge of military affairs. The new arrangement was, however, soon overtaken by international events.

The new German puppet-state had no defined borders and no constitution, and its leadership was in the hands of a German-sponsored Provisional Council of State. In response to the "Two Emperors' Declaration", a third emperor – the Russian tsar – proposed in a document of 25 December 1916 that "one of the tasks of Russia is the creation of a free Poland, comprised of the three parts that are currently divided".

The breaking of silence on the Polish Question had worldwide repercussions. In his New Year message on 22 January 1917, US president Woodrow Wilson stated the need for a united and independent Polish state, with borders stretching from the Carpathian mountains to the Baltic Sea. Meanwhile in Russia, soon after the February Revolution of 1917, the new Provisional Government announced that the rebuilding of the Polish state should be linked with a military alliance with Russia. A more concrete sign of change was the creation in France of an independent Polish army which began forming on 4 June 1917 with the approval and material support of the French president. General Józef Haller was appointed commander of the new force.

In view of these developments, the Two Emperors' Declaration of November 1916 lost its significance. Piłsudski understood this, and withdrew his co-operation from Germany and Austria. When his legionaries were ordered to swear an oath of allegiance to the German emperor most of them refused, only to be arrested and interned in prison camps; Piłsudski himself was imprisoned in Magdeburg Castle. But instead of removing Piłsudski from the scene, this turned him into a popular hero. Alarmed by the growing confidence of Polish nationalism, the Germans transformed the Provisional Council of State into a puppet "Regency Council".

WOODROW WILSON (1856–1924)

President of the United States from 1912 to 1920. It was during his term of office that the Americans entered World War I, turning the conflict decisively in favour of the Allies. His famous "Fourteen Points" declaration was an important step towards peace; the 13th point concerned the creation of an independent Poland, with access to the sea. Wilson was a friend of Ignacy Paderewski, the Polish pianist and politician, and was undoubtedly influenced by his pleas for Polish freedom.

THE LEGIONS INTERNED

Although serving as part of the Austrian army from the start of the war, Piłsudski's legionaries saw themselves as fighting against the Russians rather than for the Austrians. In July 1917 many men refused to swear an oath of allegiance to the German emperor; they were immediately sent to prison camps for the remainder of the war.

THE POLISH NATIONAL COMMITTEE

Created at Lausanne in Switzerland on 15 August 1917, the *Komitet Narodowy Polski* was intended to represent Poland in the West, and took political control of Haller's Polish Army in France. It included many important figures from the National Democracy Party, among them the committee president and founder, Roman Dmowski (*seated at centre*).

From 15 July 1917 a new body became active in Switzerland – the Polish National Committee (KNP), with Roman Dmowski at its head. It operated in France and remained the chief official body representing Poland in the international arena; it was expected to form the Polish government once the war was over.

The war finally came to an end on 11 November 1918 with the unconditional surrender of Germany. Dmowski's KNP took part in the preparation and signing in June 1919 of the Treaty of Versailles, where the victorious Allied powers created a new order in Europe. The reborn Polish state once again took its place on the map.

The cost in human lives had been high: of the two million Poles who fought in foreign armies or in Polish formations, about 400,000 became fatalities of the war.

BAYONNE COMPANY

A unit of Polish volunteers known as the Bayonne Company served as part of the 1st Regiment of the French Foreign Legion. The company fought for France in the battle for Reims in November 1914.

RUSSIAN COMMITTEE

From the beginning of World War I, Polish units fought for Russia. Among the best known were the Puławski Legion and the Krechowiecki Uhlan Regiment (named after the battle of Krechowce where they received their baptism of fire). After the February Revolution of 1917 the Supreme Polish Military Committee (NPKW, *pictured below*) was formed to oversee the recruitment of Polish units to fight alongside the Russians. Thanks to the Committee's efforts I and II Polish Corps were set up. I Corps was commanded by General Józef Dowbór-Muśnicki, who later led the Wielkopolska Rising.

THE "BLUE ARMY" IN FRANCE

In June 1917 a Polish army was set up in France with the full approval of the French authorities. By 1918 it numbered 100,000 soldiers, recruited mainly from Polish emigrés and prisoners of war captured from the Austrian and German armies. Its equipment and famous blue uniforms were supplied by the French. Its commander was General Józef Haller, who swore his oath of allegiance on 6 October 1918. When World War I ended Haller's "Blue Army" returned to its newly independent Polish homeland.

LENIN'S REVOLUTION AND POLAND

In October 1917 the Russian empire fell apart as the Bolsheviks (or communists), led by Vladimir Lenin, seized power. In August 1918 the Bolsheviks annulled the treaties which had allowed the partitioning of Poland. The fate of the Russian revolution hung in the balance throughout 1919; Piłsudski was, however, not prepared to side with the "White" opponents of the communists, fearing they would restore Poland's pre-war status as a province of the Russian empire.

POLAND
REBORN

THE STRUGGLE FOR POLAND'S BORDERS

In October 1918, with all three of the Partitioning Powers – Germany, Austria and Russia – on the verge of collapse, Poland's dream of independence became reality. But huge questions remained: who would rule the country, and where would its frontiers lie?

As World War I neared its end the German and Austro–Hungarian empires, exhausted by four years of conflict, began to fall apart. The Russian empire had already collapsed in 1917, engulfing the country in a tragic civil war. Poles in all three Partitions at last had the chance for rebuilding an independent Polish state, free from the fear of foreign intervention.

IGNACY JAN PADEREWSKI (1860–1941)

A world-famous pianist and composer, his influence on the political stage contributed greatly to international awareness of the Polish Question. From late 1918 until 27 November 1919 he served as Poland's premier and as minister of foreign affairs.

A HERO'S RETURN
Paderewski's arrival in Poznań on 26 December 1918 was the signal for an uprising in Wielkopolska.

The immediate question was, who would rule the country? In the confusion at least four bodies claimed to represent the Polish government. The first of them, in

JÓZEF PIŁSUDSKI (1867–1935)

Born in Lithuania, he was convicted in 1887 for conspiring to assassinate Tsar Alexander III and spent five years in Siberia. On release he determined to seize independence by force, and set up a para-military branch of the Polish Socialist Party. From the outbreak of World War I he commanded the 1st Brigade of the Legions in Austrian service, but was arrested in 1917 when he refused to serve the Germans. Freed in November 1918, he returned to Warsaw and briefly took command of the reborn Polish state as its "Leader". A military coup in 1926 returned him to the forefront of Polish politics.

IGNACY DASZYŃSKI (1866–1936)

Politician and labour activist. A close wartime associate of Piłsudski, he became premier of the provisional government on 6/7 November 1918. Piłsudski entrusted him with forming a permanent government on 14 November, but he proved unequal to the task and was replaced on 18 November.

Paris, was the Polish National Committee led by Roman Dmowski, which conducted negotiations with the Western powers as Poland's representatives. In the former Austrian zone, power was in the hands the Polish Liquidation Commission (formed in Kraków on 28 October) and of the "Provisional People's Government of the Polish Republic" (formed in Lublin on 6/7 November). Meanwhile, in the former Russian zone which had been overrun by Germany's armies, the German-appointed Regency Council were rapidly losing their grip on power as the political situation deteriorated and Bolshevik cells called for revolution in Warsaw.

The confusion was resolved when Józef Piłsudski suddenly appeared on the scene. Released from a German jail in Magdeburg, he reached Warsaw on 10 November. The Regency Council handed over command of the army to him on the following day, and gave him the remainder of its powers on 14 November, before disbanding itself. Piłsudski appeased the Provisional Government in Lublin by asking its premier, Ignacy Daszyński, to form a new cabinet. At the end of the month a decree outlined the political structure of the new state and gave it the official title of the Republic of Poland. The arrangement did not suit everyone – not least Dmowski, who believed that his Polish National Committee had the legal right to govern Poland. Dmowski became Piłsudski's most outspoken opponent.

The key problem that now faced Piłsudski was the demarcation of Poland's new frontiers. Despite the horrendous casualties of World War I, Poland's neighbours were reluctant to give up territory without a fight. Disturbances in the former German Partition began soon after German troops withdrew from Warsaw on 11 November 1918. When the internationally renowned pianist Ignacy Paderewski arrived in Poznań in December, pro-Polish demonstrations began and soon turned into an full-scale armed revolt known as the Wielkopolska Rising. Fighting continued until 18 February 1919. Finally, by the terms of the Versailles Treaty signed on 28 June 1919, Poland was given Wielkopolska almost in its entirety.

Poland's claims to Danzig (Gdańsk) were settled without armed conflict. Danzig, though populated mainly by

STANISŁAW TACZAK (1874–1960)

A veteran of Piłsudski's Legions, he led the Wielkopolska Rising from 28 December 1918 to 15 January 1919, and commanded an infantry brigade in the restored Polish Army. After the 1939 campaign against Germany, he was interned for the whole of World War II.

JÓZEF DOWBÓR- -MUŚNICKI (1867–1937)

Commander of I Polish Corps in Russia from 1917 to 1918, he helped organize the "Armia Wielkopolska" during the Wielkopolska Rising, and took over command from Taczak after January 1919. He was instrumental in turning the rebel forces into a regular army.

WOJCIECH KORFANTY (1873–1939)

Photographed here (*seated third from left*) among the Polish commissioners of the Upper Silesian Plebiscite, Korfanty was a political and social activist. One of the first Polish representatives ever to be elected to the German Reichstag, he was strongly pro-Polish in his views and became a figurehead during the Silesian Risings of 1920–21. In 1922 he joined the Christian Democrats and went on to became president of the National Council. An opponent of Piłsudski's *Sanacja* regime, he was imprisoned in 1930, and later escaped to Czechoslovakia.

The battle at Góra Świętej Anny (Annenberg, 21–27 May 1921) was the largest action of the Third Silesian Rising. The hill was a key strategic point, slowing the German advance. In the end the Germans took the position, but with crippling losses.

German-speakers, had for centuries been part of the Polish Commonwealth and Poland's main seaport. By stressing its importance at Versailles, Polish diplomats managed to have it declared a Free City – belonging neither to Poland nor to Germany. Poland received the right to use the port, as well as to run the post office and supervise the rail system. As further compensation Poland received a narrow strip of land known as the "Polish Corridor" which connected Poland to a short stretch of Baltic coastline. This, however, cut off Danzig and East Prussia from German territory. It was not a happy solution, as the events of 1939 were later to show.

At the Versailles Conference it was also decided that the national status of Upper Silesia was to be determined by a vote of the entire population, a so-called Plebiscite*. This went against the wishes of both Polish and German-speaking Silesians. Public demonstrations followed, precipitating a general strike on 11 August 1919 after seven miners were shot at Mysłowice. On the night of 16/17 August the strike escalated into what is now termed the First Silesian Rising. Within ten days the rising had been brutally put down by the German authorities. French, Italian and British troops arrived to stabilize the situation,

GERMANS OR SILESIANS?

In March 1921 thousands of Germans journeyed from all over the Reich to vote on the national status of Upper Silesia. Special trains were laid on from many German stations (here Berlin). Poles were convinced that many of these travellers had no legal right to vote.

* Words marked by an asterisk are explained in the glossary on pages 124–125.

and to oversee the activities of the Plebiscite Commission. One of the main bones of contention to Polish-speaking Silesians was the heavy-handedness of the German security police (Sipo). Their terror tactics provoked the Second Rising, which broke out on the night of 19/20 August 1920. After six days the head of the Polish Plebiscite Commission, Wojciech Korfanty, called a halt to the fighting. As part of the peace settlement, a new German–Polish police force replaced the Sipo.

O gizdy! To wy ze swoimi miljonami uciekacie do Holandji, a my mamy za was płacić długi? Niema głupich!

My głosujemy za Polską!

Ihr deutschen Hallunken! Ihr flüchtet mit euern Schätzen nach Holland und wir sollen wohl für euch die Milliardenschulden zahlen? Nein!

Wir stimmen für Polen!

WE'RE VOTING FOR POLAND!

The referendum (Plebiscite) for Upper Silesia saw much virulent propaganda such as this poster. The Germans promised that when joined with Germany Upper Silesia would see civil order and economic progress restored. The Poles underlined the fact that Silesia had for many centuries belonged to Poland, and claimed that economic progress would be hindered as businessmen fled to shelter their money in Holland.

The Plebiscite vote finally took place on 20 March 1921. The Germans took great pains to win. After intensive propaganda, nearly 200,000 ostensible "citizens of Silesia" were transported from all over Germany to vote; predictably, the Plebiscite went in favour of Germany. But the Poles refused to accept defeat. Another general strike followed on 2 May 1921, leading directly to the Third Silesian Rising which broke out on the same evening with the seizure of key communications centres.

The third rising was by far the most violent of the Silesian disturbances. Pitched battles were fought at Góra Świętej Anny, Gliwice and Kędzierzyn. Finally, on 5 July, convinced that the Plebiscite vote indeed needed to be reconsidered, French, British and Italian troops of the Interallied Commission arrived to separate the rival factions. In October 1921 the League of Nations divided Upper Silesia into two parts, and later confirmed their decision in mid-1922. About 30 percent of the area, with half the population, became part of Poland. The major towns of Gliwice (Gleiwitz), Zabrze (Hindenburg), and Bytom (Beuthen) remained in Germany, along with about 500,000 Polish-speaking Silesians. Poland got the bulk of the coalfields, along with Katowice (Kattowitz) and Chorzów (Königshütte). It was a settlement that neither side liked, but it was, at last, a settlement.

Meanwhile, on 11 July 1920, a similar Plebiscite on the national status of East Prussia had gone ahead in relative peace. Amid allegations of German pressure on voters and the importation of thousands of "outvoters" from the Reich, the Poles took just 2.2 percent of the vote. Poland was duly awarded just eight border villages, and the bulk of the disputed area became part of Germany.

In the south, the demarcation of Poland's borders with the old Austro–Hungarian Empire was to end in bloodshed. One of the by-products of World War I had been the creation of the new state of Czechoslovakia. The new Polish–Czech border ran for much of its length along the ridge of the Carpathian mountains – here there was no dispute. More problematic were three lowland gaps at Cieszyn/Tesin, Orawa/Orava and Spisz/Spis. Despite large Polish minorities, the Allied Powers decided that both Spisz and Orawa should end up mostly in Czechoslovakia. Cieszyn evoked greater emotions. In November 1918 the local communities had come to a friendly agreement on where the new border should lie. The Prague government disapproved, and in January 1919 sent in troops to seize the area. Fighting broke out, followed by 18 months of chaos. Finally, in July 1920, a neutral Council of Ambassadors awarded Czechoslovakia the larger half of the Duchy of Cieszyn and two-thirds of the inhabitants; the entire Zaolzie region of the duchy, with nearly 150,000 Polish-speakers, became part of Czechoslovakia.

In the east, the marking out of Poland's new frontier with Russia was to be by far the most violent of the border disputes, leading to a full-scale war which lasted nearly two years. At the Paris Conference Dmowski had pleaded for the restoration of Poland's pre-partition borders of 1772, but nothing could be settled while the Russian Civil War was in progress. Piłsudski dreamed of forming Poland, Lithuania, Byelorussia, Ukraine and Finland into a federation, hoping that together these states could stand against the might of Russia. Such ideas aroused fear of a return to the excesses of the 17th--century Polish–Lithuanian Commonwealth and, in the end, nothing came of them.

Piłsudski's answer was to seize the disputed territories while Russia remained weak. In late April 1919 Polish troops captured Wilno from the Red Army. Soon after, a Polish offensive into Ukraine began. By early May 1920 Polish troops were in the capital, Kiev, which they

THE "MIRACLE ON THE VISTULA"

In July 1920 volunteers assembled in Warsaw (*photo*) ready to defend the capital from the advancing Red Army. The first Soviet assaults on Warsaw (13–15 August) were repulsed. A daring Polish counterattack on 16 August cut supply lines, and by 18 August the Soviets were surrounded and completely defeated.

Baltic Sea

Gdynia

Danzig (Gdańsk)

Königsberg (Kró

Elbing (Elbląg)

EAST PR

"POLISH CORRIDOR"

Chojnice

Allenstein (Olsz

Bydgoszcz

Toruń

Poznań

POLAND

W

Raszyn

Kalisz

Łódź

Rad

GERMANY

Częstochowa

Kielce

CENTR

Katowice

Kraków

Bielsko

Wieliczka

Cieszyn

Jas

CZECHOSLOVAKIA

THE SECOND POLISH REPUBLIC, 1918–1939

Poland's frontiers were determined between 1918 and 1922, althou powers did not recognize the eastern border with the USSR until 1

Free City of Danzig (Gdańsk)

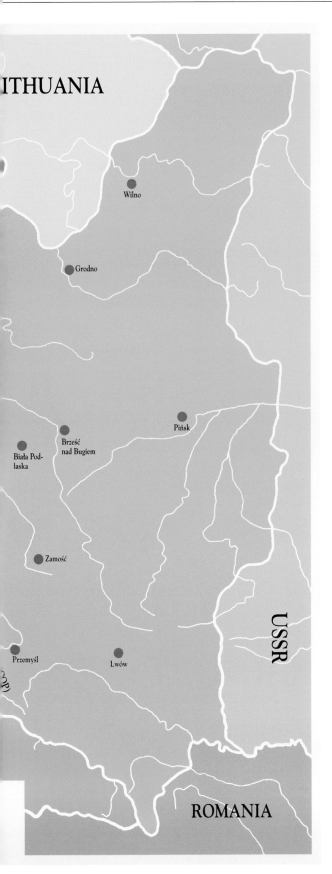

handed over to the town's citizens. In the meantime the Soviet Army gathered its forces and went on the counteroffensive. The Polish army fell back in some disorder, and before long the Russians were near Warsaw.

Then an event known as the "Miracle on the Vistula" happened. In one brilliant tactical stroke (13–16 August 1920) Piłsudski outflanked the overextended Russian armies. With their supply lines cut, the Soviets were forced to retreat or be surrounded. Further well-timed offensives soon had the Soviets in full flight. Lenin sued for peace, and at Riga on 18 March 1921 the new Polish–Soviet border was agreed. Piłsudski's Lithuanian home town of Wilno remained Polish.

The newly won borders of 1921 gave Poland an area of about 390,000 km^2, inhabited by some 27 million people. The territorial disputes were, however, not over. Germany, in particular, remained resentful of the decisions of the Versailles Treaty.

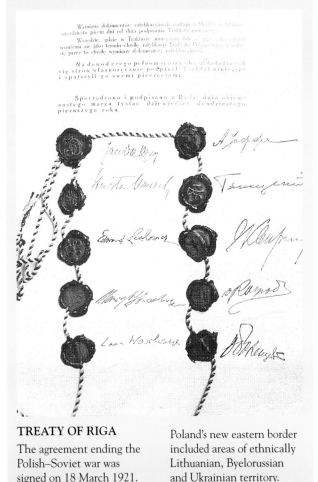

TREATY OF RIGA

The agreement ending the Polish–Soviet war was signed on 18 March 1921.

Poland's new eastern border included areas of ethnically Lithuanian, Byelorussian and Ukrainian territory.

BETWEEN THE WARS – THE SECOND POLISH REPUBLIC

The task of rebuilding Poland was to be difficult. The physical destruction of World War I was repaired, but political life became chaotic and the economy suffered. When Piłsudski seized power in the May Coup of 1926 he enjoyed widespread public support.

When Poland achieved independence in 1918, many Western leaders did not believe it would survive for long as a sovereign power. The challenges facing the new state were enormous. Huge differences existed between the former Russian, German and Austrian territories, not least the three separate dialects and different attitudes and habits which had sprung up during 123 years of foreign rule. "Prussian Poles" were suspicious of "Russian Poles", who were suspicious of "Austrian Poles": each had their own way of doing things. Even the rail systems were of different gauges.

Nearly one-third of Poland's 27 million citizens belonged to ethnic minorities: Ukrainians (14 percent), Jews (10 percent), Byelorussians (3 percent) and Germans (2.5 percent). Each had their own political aspirations, which often conflicted with those of the increasingly nationalistic Polish majority.

An important landmark was the Polish Republic's new Constitution, laid in place in March 1921. Based on that of France, it created a Seym of 444 seats elected by proportional representation, and a Senate of 111 seats. In practice most power was in the hands of the Seym; the Senate was restricted to ratifying new laws, while the President was seen mainly as a figurehead who was to represent Poland abroad.

Józef Piłsudski was Head of State (*Naczelnik*) from 1919, but refused to stand in the first presidential elections in 1922 on the grounds that the post carried too little power. Instead Professor Gabriel Narutowicz was elected. Criticized by nationalists for winning as a result of votes cast by "non-Poles", he was assassinated a few days after taking office. His successor was Stanisław Wojciechowski. Piłsudski, for the time being, withdrew from public life, to a quiet rural estate at Sulejówek just outside Warsaw.

The young democracy soon started to founder. The economic situation deteriorated and inflation began to run out of control. Bickering between the parties caused

PIŁSUDSKI REMEMBERED

The most important figure of the interwar years – Marshal Józef Piłsudski, the "Naczelnik" or Leader of Poland – was referred to by the post-war communist government only rarely and reluctantly. It was not until 12 May 1995 that the Seym corrected this injustice during the celebrations on the 60th anniversary of his death, in the following statement:

"Józef Piłsudski will remain in the memory of our nation as the founder of independence and as the victorious leader who fended off a foreign assault that threatened the whole of Europe and its civilization.
Józef Piłsudski served his motherland well, and has entered our history forever."

GABRIEL NARUTOWICZ (1865–1922)

The first President of the Second Polish Republic. Shortly after his December 1922 inauguration Piłsudski greeted Narutowicz with the following words:
"Mr President, I feel unusually happy to be the first person in Poland to have the great honour of receiving in my house and in the presence of my family, the first citizen of the Polish Republic....
As the only Polish officer currently in service who, until now, has never stood to attention before anybody, I stand thus to attention before Poland which You represent, offering a toast – Long live the first President of the Republic!"
Piłsudski's high spirits did not last long: on 16 December, while visiting an exhibition at the Zachęta Art Gallery in Warsaw, Narutowicz was assassinated – just two days after taking power.

USTAWA Z DNIA 17 MARCA 1921 ROKU

KONSTYTUCJA RZECZYPOSPOLITEJ POLSKIEJ

W IMIĘ BOGA WSZECHMOGĄCEGO!
MY, NARÓD POLSKI, dziękując OPATRZNOŚCI za wyzwolenie nas z półtorawiekowej niewoli, wspominając z wdzięcznością męstwo i wytrwałość ofiarnej walki pokoleń, które najlepsze wysiłki swoje sprawie niepodległości bez przerwy poświęcały, nawiązując do świetnej tradycji wiekopomnej Konstytucji 3-go Maja – dobro całej, zjednoczonej i niepodległej Matki-Ojczyzny mając na oku, a pragnąc Jej byt niepodległy, potęgę i bezpieczeństwo oraz ład społeczny utwierdzić na wiekuistych zasadach prawa i wolności, pragnąc zarazem zapewnić rozwój wszystkich Jej sił moralnych i materjalnych dla dobra całej odradzającej się ludzkości, wszystkim obywatelom Rzeczypospolitej równość, a pracy poszanowanie, należne prawa i szczególną opiekę Państwa zabezpieczyć – tę oto Ustawę Konstytucyjną na Sejmie Ustawodawczym Rzeczypospolitej Polskiej uchwalamy i stanowimy.

The opening page of the so-called March Constitution, authorized on 17 March 1921. It gave wide rights to all the citizens of the Polish Republic.

EXCERPTS FROM THE 1921 CONSTITUTION

Article 2
Overall rule of the Polish Republic belongs to the Nation. The organs of state in the field of legislation are the Seym and the Senate; in the field of executive power, the President of the Polish Republic along with the responsible ministers; in the field of the administration of justice, the independent Courts.
Article 25
The President of the Republic calls together, opens, adjourns and closes the Seym and the Senate.
Article 45
The President of the Republic appoints and dismisses the Premier of the Council of Ministers, (and) on his recommendation nominates and dismisses Ministers.

EXCERPTS FROM THE 1935 CONSTITUTION

Article 1
The Polish state is the collective property of all its citizens (…)
Article 2
At the head of the state stands the President of the Republic. On him falls the responsibility before God and history for the destiny of the state (…) In his person is concentrated the singular and indivisible authority of the State.
Article 12
The President of the Republic appoints at his discretion the Premier of the Council of Ministers, and on his recommendation the Ministers; he convenes and dissolves the Seym and the Senate; is the overall chief of the Armed Forces; represents the State abroad, receives representatives of foreign powers and sends abroad representatives of the Polish State; decides questions of war and peace; concludes and ratifies agreements with other states; appoints state officials in posts consigned to Him.

The above extracts from the March 1921 and April 1935 Constitutions demonstrate the increasingly dictatorial nature of government during the interwar years. The President, in particular, was given far wider powers.

STANISŁAW WOJCIECHOWSKI
(1869–1953) – President of Poland from 1922 to 1926.

THE POLISH CABINET
In June 1926 the Cabinet debated alterations to the Constitution in the Royal Castle in Warsaw. These reduced the powers of the Seym and greatly increased those of the president.

the government to fall repeatedly. Widespread demonstrations brought the country to the verge of chaos.

On 12 May 1926, amid mounting disorder, Piłsudski decided that he could stand by no longer. Gathering a group of devoted officers and their regiments, he marched on the nation's capital. At the Poniatowski Bridge in Warsaw, Piłsudski had a tense encounter with President Wojciechowski who asked him to turn back. He refused. Forces loyal to the government put up resistance, but reinforcements failed to reach Warsaw since Piłsudski's supporters had paralysed the rail system. After three days of street battles, President Wojciechowski and Premier

Wincenty Witos stood down; full-scale civil war was narrowly averted. Piłsudski's "May Coup" had succeeded because a large section of Polish society desperately wanted a change for the better.

Despite his victory Piłsudski turned down the presidency. On his personal recommendation, the post went instead to a professor of chemistry, Ignacy Mościcki. Piłsudski briefly held the premiership, but refused to get involved in party politics. He maintained an aloof but paternal eye on the fortunes of the country. Convinced that his key role was with the army, it was to be as "the Marshal" that he was afterwards fondly remembered.

The watchword of the new era was *Sanacja*, meaning "return to health", both political and moral. The government was in need of a thorough clean-up, and this it got. The plethora of political parties, which had been such a hindrance to effective government, were tamed – some by force. Outspoken opponents of the new regime such as Witos and Korfanty were bundled into prison or forced into exile.

On 12 May 1935 Józef Piłsudski died. It was a personal loss to millions who saw him as the father of the nation. After a magnificent state funeral, his body was laid to rest on the Wawel Hill in Kraków and his heart was placed in his beloved Wilno. A few weeks before his death a new Constitution had been approved in April 1935. It strengthened the position of the government and gave greater powers to President Mościcki. The leading post in the country, after the presidency itself, went to Piłsudski's old comrade-in-arms General Edward Rydz-Śmigły, who succeeded as General Inspector of the Armed Forces. Rule was now effectively in the hands of "the colonels" – a clique of army officers. Yet, despite the outward signs of being a military dictatorship, the Polish spirit and traditional defiance of authority ensured that Poland remained a relatively liberal state.

The 1930s brought a new danger – the rise of fascism in Germany. Adolf Hitler, the leader of the National Socialist (Nazi) party, seized power in 1933. His aim was to turn Germany into a world power, at the cost of the Slavs whom he regarded as fit only to be slaves in his new Third Reich. When Hitler annexed Austria in March 1938 and parts of Czechoslovakia in October 1938, it

PONIATOWSKI BRIDGE
It was on this Warsaw bridge on 12 May 1926 that the dramatic confrontation between Piłsudski and President

Wojciechowski took place. Piłsudski refused to turn back, and his troops marched into Warsaw, taking the town after three days of fighting.

looked as though Poland was next on the menu. Meanwhile, in the east, the Russian bear was awakening under its tyrannical leader Jozef Stalin. Poland's only option was to seek strong allies. Polish foreign minister Józef Beck renewed alliances with France and Britain, not knowing how much they would really be worth when put to the test. As extra insurance, non-aggression pacts were signed with Germany and the USSR.

In October 1938, increasingly sure of himself, Hitler proposed a new deal with Poland to replace the Versailles Treaty. By its terms the Free City of Danzig (Gdańsk) was to become part of Germany, and new *Autobahn* and rail routes were to cross the "Polish Corridor" linking East Prussia with Germany. On 5 May 1939 Józef Beck turned down the proposals. Few doubted what the following months would bring, and the nation began to prepare for war. Many Poles offered treasured possessions, jewellery

IGNACY MOŚCICKI (1867–1946)
A chemist by profession, he was Poland's president from 1926 to 1939.

EDWARD RYDZ-ŚMIGŁY (1886–1941)
Piłsudski's right-hand man, he became Marshal of Poland in November 1936.

BELVEDERE PALACE

Built in Warsaw between 1818 and 1822, this was Poland's official state residence from 1918. Between 1926 and 1935 it was the abode of Marshal Józef Piłsudski.

THE SEYM OF THE SECOND REPUBLIC

The Constitution of 1935 reduced the Seym from 444 deputies to 208, making it more manageable. Today's Seym sessions take place in the same semi-circular chamber.

JÓZEF BECK'S SPEECH

On 5 May 1935 the Polish minister for foreign affairs, Józef Beck, gave an important speech turning down German demands regarding the Free City of Danzig (Gdańsk) and the "Polish Corridor". From the speaker's rostrum in the Seym he delivered the following momentous lines: *"We in Poland do not understand the concept of peace at any price. There is only one thing in the life of people, nations, and states which is priceless, and that thing is honour."*

and family heirlooms to help re-equip the armed forces. Few suspected that they would have to fight not just Hitler's storm troops, but the Red Army as well. On 23 August 1939 Nazi Germany and Soviet Russia signed the Molotov–Ribbentrop Pact, secretly agreeing that after Poland's defeat her territories were to be divided between them along the line of Narew, Vistula and San rivers. In effect, it was the fourth Partition of Poland.

POLAND INVADES CZECHOSLOVAKIA

The border town of Cieszyn and the nearby Zaolzie district had been a bone of contention between Poland and Czechoslovakia since 1919. Just as Germany, Italy, France and Britain were talking of partitioning the Czechoslovak state, the Polish government made one of its greatest errors of the interwar years. On 2 October 1938 Polish Army units under General Bortnowski occupied the Zaolzie. This rash move led to accusations of open co-operation with Nazi Germany.

infantryman and uhlan of the Polish Army in the 1930s

POLES AT HOME AND ABROAD IN WORLD WAR II

On 1 September 1939 German forces invaded Poland, starting history's greatest conflict – World War II. From its first day to the last, Poles fought the enemy on land, sea and air, on all fronts at home and overseas.

The opening action of World War II was the September 1939 campaign. Poland's armed forces were outclassed by the Nazi war machine, but at actions like Modlin, Westerplatte and the defence of the naval base at Hel they put up stiff resistance. In the battle of Bzura (Kutno) the Polish army even launched a counterattack which delayed the German advance by several days. In truth, Poland had little hope of winning on her own against Germany. The original war plan had been to resist the Nazi onslaught for two weeks, giving France and Britain time to attack in the West. However, this support, promised by treaty, never came.

The death blow came on 17 September 1939. With Poland's armed forces fully engaged against the Germans, the USSR invaded from the east. It was a stab in the back, from which there was absolutely no hope of recovery. Even so, the 1939 campaign lasted six weeks, and for the Germans it was far from the "light manoeuvres" they had expected. In all they suffered 16,000 killed and 32,000 wounded, as well as losing 674 tanks and 564 aircraft. Hitler's plan of action in the West had to be postponed for months while his forces were rebuilt.

Polish losses were, of course, much higher, and more were to die during the six years of occupation. Many Polish troops had the misfortune to surrender to the Russians. Along with nearly two million Polish civilians they were sent to camps deep in the Soviet Union. Polish officers were separated at an early stage, and about 14,000 were murdered in one of the darkest deeds of the Stalinist era – Katyń.

On the fall of Poland about 90,000 Polish troops had managed to escape over the border into Romania and

PZL P–37B "ŁOŚ" BOMBER

The superiority of the German *Luftwaffe* was a major cause of Poland's defeat in 1939. The Polish Airforce had barely 400 aircraft – most of them obsolete – facing more than 2,000 German machines. Nevertheless, the *Łoś* (Elk) bomber, built by the rapidly developing Polish aviation industry, was one of the best aircraft of its type in the world. It could fly at 445km per hour and carry 3000 kg of bombs; but only 36 were in service by September 1939.

THE KATYŃ GRAVES

On 13 April 1943 Berlin radio announced the discovery of mass graves near Smolensk in Russia. They proved to be the resting place of up to 14,000 Polish officers and civil officials captured by the Soviets in 1939 and later executed by the secret police. On 13 April 1990 the Russian authorities officially admitted to the killings.

THE POLISH NAVY

Poland began the war with a small but modern navy of three destroyers and five submarines plus smaller vessels. Forewarned of Hitler's plans, they were able to escape to Britain on the outbreak of war. From the beginning these warships operated alongside the Royal Navy and were involved in convoy escort and a range of other duties. During the war Polish ships (and replacements provided by the Allies) sank 12 enemy warships and 41 merchant vessels, and shot down 24 aircraft. Especially distinguished was the destroyer ORP *Błyskawica*. After returning to Poland in 1947, she remained in service for many years.

WŁADYSŁAW SIKORSKI (1881–1943)

Premier of the Polish Government-in-exile from 1939, and commander-in-chief of Polish Armed Forces in the West from the same year. He died in a mysterious air-crash near Gibraltar in 1943.

WŁADYSŁAW RACZKIEWICZ (1885–1947)

Marshal of the Senate from 1930 to 1935. With the internment of President Mościcki after the 1939 Campaign, Raczkiewicz was appointed President of the Polish Government-in-exile, based in London.

THE POLISH AIRFORCE

Serving with the Royal Air Force in 1940, the Polish 302 and 303 Fighter Squadrons were put on active status after Lt. Ludwik Paszkiewicz shot down a German Dornier while on a training mission. With a reputation for reckless bravery, Polish pilots played a key role in the Battle of Britain, 303 Squadron (*badge, left*) gaining more air kills than any other squadron during the battle. In five years of war Polish aces, such as Stanisław Skalski and Witold Urbanowicz, shot down 809 enemy aircraft and 190 V-1 flying bombs.

Hungary. Most made their way to France or Syria, where the Polish Armed Forces were reformed. By May 1940 there were 84,500 Poles under arms in the West; their long wanderings around Europe earned them the nickname "Sikorski's tourists". The first of them to see action again was the Independent Podhalańska Rifle Brigade. Formed in France, it was shipped to the aid of Norway in April 1940 and distinguished itself at Narvik. When the German "Lightning War" on France began, Polish troops helped in its defence. France was, however, quickly over-run. Several Polish formations escaped to Switzerland where they were interned. Just 24,000 Polish troops were successfully evacuated to Great Britain, the only European power still resisting Germany.

Scotland now became the main wartime base of the Polish Armed Forces in the West. Here, organized as Polish 1st Corps, they were deployed to defend eastern Scotland in the event of a German invasion from Norway. Many Polish formations, including 1st Independent Parachute Brigade and 1st Armoured Division, received their training in Scotland. Further south, in England, Polish pilots helped defend the skies from the German *Luftwaffe*. Their combat experience, won so dearly in Poland and France, proved of great value to the RAF, and

POLISH ARMOUR

1st Armoured Division under General Stanisław Maczek was Poland's largest tank formation of the war. Formed in Scotland in 1942, it was equipped with British Cromwell tanks (*above*) and American Shermans. Shipped to France in July 1944, it was instrumental in the closing of the "Falaise Pocket", helped liberate Belgium and Holland, and in May 1945, accepted the surrender of the German naval base at Wilhelmshaven.

helped prevent Hitler from gaining the superiority in the air necessary for the launching of a seaborne invasion of Britain. With the Battle of Britain won, Polish bomber squadrons would later help carry the fight to the industrial plants and cities of Germany.

After Germany's surprise invasion of Russia on 22 June 1941, the Soviet government hurriedly re-established diplomatic relations with the Polish government-in-exile (30 July 1941). Desperate for troops to halt

AUSCHWITZ (OŚWIĘCIM)
One of the greatest crimes of humanity took place near the small Polish town of Oświęcim, 60km west of Kraków. In their Final Solution to the "Jewish problem", the Nazis perfected death factories to exterminate Jews and other victims, with industrial efficiency. Millions were murdered, at this and other camps on Polish soil.

MONTE CASSINO
World War II's greatest feat of Polish arms took place at the monastery on Monte Cassino in Italy. Poles of Anders' 2nd Corps reached the summit on 18 May 1944 after suffering about 3,500 casualties.

POLISH–SOVIET PACT
In London on 30 July 1941, General Sikorski and the Soviet ambassador Ivan Maiski signed a treaty restoring diplomatic relations which had been broken off after Russia's invasion of Poland in 1939. The document authorized co-operation in the war against Germany. Work began in Russia to recruit a Polish army. In 1942 these troops, under General Władysław Anders, left Russia via Iran to fight alongside the British Army in Italy.

POLAND UNDER NAZI OCCUPATION, 1939–1944
- ○ main concentration camps and death camps
- — Poland's borders on 1 September 1939

Baltic

Danzig (Gdańsk)
Sztutowo (Stutthof)
LITHUANIA
Olsztyn (Allenstein)
Toruń
Treblinka
Poznań
Warsaw
Chełmno
GERMAN REICH
Sobibór
Majdanek
GENERAL-GOUVERNEMENT
Bełżec
Oświęcim (Auschwitz)
Kraków
Lwów
USSR
PROTECTORATE OF BOHEMIA & MORAVIA
SLOVAKIA
HUNGARY
ROMANIA

— temporary German–Soviet border (28 September 1939 – 22 June 1941)

BERLING'S ARMY
In 1943 Polish troops were raised in the USSR, under the command of a Polish communist, Zygmunt Berling (1896–1980). With Russian equipment (such as the T-34 tanks, *above*) they fought alongside the Red Army in the liberation of Poland.

Hitler's advancing armies, Stalin agreed to the formation of a Polish army in Russia under General Władysław Anders. More than 60,000 Polish soldiers – most of them prisoners of the 1939 campaign – were concentrated in central Russia; but because of difficulties in supplying them with weapons and even food, Stalin reluctantly allowed them to leave for Iran, along with their families, in 1942. In Iran and Palestine Anders' men were re-organized under British supervision to become 2nd Polish Corps. Shipped to Italy at the end of 1943, the corps distinguished itself as part of the British 8th Army, particularly in the costly battle for Monte Cassino (May 1944).

The Allies landed back on the European mainland on D-Day, 6 June 1944. Among the Polish units that advanced through France and the Low Countries and on to Germany was Polish 1st Armoured Division. Also present was 1st Independent Parachute Brigade; although trained to fight in the liberation of Poland, it was air-dropped in September 1944 at Arnhem in Holland.

Back in Poland, a resistance movement had sprung up soon after the country's surrender. In 1942 this was organized into the Home Army (*Armia Krajowa* or AK). It was by far the largest underground organization in the Nazi-occupied countries. The AK fought an aggressive partisan war, tying down a large army of occupation; and achieved successes in intelligence gathering – for example, supplying Britain with information on the V-2 rocket.

A second attempt to organize Polish units in Soviet Russia was directed by Polish communists such as General Zygmunt Berling. The first formed was 1st Kościuszko Infantry Division, which suffered heavy losses when sent prematurely into battle at Lenino in October 1943. By 1944 Polish forces in the USSR had expanded with the creation of the 1st and 2nd Armies. These fought alongside the Red Army as it advanced into Poland and then on to Germany; Polish troops were present in Berlin when, on 8 May 1945, the Third Reich surrendered unconditionally, bringing the war in Europe to an end.

Proportionately, Poland lost more than any other participant of World War II: six million Polish citizens were killed, cities were devastated, hundreds of years of human endeavour wiped out. If this was not enough, in the interests of *realpolitik*, the Western powers abandoned Poland to the Russian sphere of influence.

THE WARSAW UPRISING

The most famous and most tragic enterprise of the Polish Home Army (AK) began on 1 August 1944, and was expected to last ten days – plenty of time for the Red Army to reach the city. On Stalin's order, however, the Soviets cynically did not intervene. Support from the Allies, who were denied the use of Russian airstrips, was limited to air drops of supplies, most of which fell into German hands.

In intense street-fighting German troops eliminated Polish-held pockets of the city block by block. Two thousand AK men and women escaped through the city sewers (as commemorated in the monument, *above*). Finally, on 2 October, the rising's 63rd day, AK commander Gen. Tadeusz Bór-Komorowski surrendered. The rising had cost 200,000 lives, mostly civilians. When it was over, Hitler ordered Warsaw "razed without trace".

IN THE RUINS OF BERLIN

After desperate fighting, the Soviet and Polish armies captured Hitler's capital on 2 May 1945. Here Poles are seen on more leisurely duties shortly after the city's fall.

MODERN POLAND – FROM COMMUNISM TO INDEPENDENCE

The joy at Poland's liberation after World War II soon turned sour as Stalin imposed his brutal regime. It was not until the 1980s and the rise of Solidarity that a bright shaft of light broke through the grey gloom of communist rule.

The communists took power in Poland not through a popular revolution, but with military muscle-power. In mid-1944, after pushing the Germans out of Russia, the Soviet Army along with units of the communist-led Polish People's Army crossed the pre-war Polish frontier. In an operation known as *Burza* (Tempest) the Polish Home Army (AK) attempted to speed Poland's liberation. They sabotaged German lines of communication and harried German attempts at resisting the Soviet advance.

Yet such combined operations with the Russians did not last. Soviet troops had orders to disarm all Home Army men and to arrest any who resisted. Some were later transported to camps in the USSR; many were murdered. Alongside the Red Army came detachments of the Soviet security service, the NKVD, who systematically sought out and eliminated Polish nationalists.

Stalin had no intention of letting the Poles take power for themselves. In Moscow on 20 July 1944 he set up the Polish Committee of National Liberation (PKWN) to take control in the recaptured Polish territories. PKWN's manifesto and structure were not finalized until mid-August, but all documents were printed in Moscow and falsely redated 21 and 22 July, and said to have been signed at Chełm Lubelski, the first Polish town liberated west of the Curzon Line*. PKWN eventually set up base in Lublin and, as Poland's new governing body, became known as the Lublin Committee.

Meanwhile the fight against the communists turned into a minor civil war. Although the Home Army was officially disbanded by its commander General Leopold Okulicki on 19 January 1945, many of its members remained active in an association called "Freedom and Independence" (Wolność i Niezawisłość). They fought alongside two other anti-communist organizations, the National Armed Forces (NSZ) and NIE – literally "No" (to communist rule). In March the Soviet authorities arranged a meeting with Polish underground leaders. Those who turned up were arrested and taken to the Lubianka prison in Moscow, where confessions were beaten out of them. In the "Trial of the 16" – which lasted just six days (16–21 June) – they were charged with collaborating with the Nazis. The senior among them received sentences of five to ten years, although many were never released: General Okulicki was murdered in prison.

STANISŁAW MIKOŁAJCZYK (1901–1966)

Vice-president of the Peasant Party in the 1930s, he became vice-premier in the London government-in-exile in 1940 and premier from 1943. The only prominent figure to return to Poland after the war, he was made vice-premier in the Provisional Government. Realising that his life was in danger, he fled to London after the rigged 1947 elections.

LAND FOR THE PEOPLE

On 6 September 1944 the Lublin Committee issued a decree intended to destroy the Polish landed aristocracy. Estates larger than 50 hectares were nationalized, as was property owned by Germans and wartime collaborators. Many of these plots were divided up and given to peasants, but because of their small size they proved to be inefficient as farms.

* Words marked by an asterisk are explained in the glossary on pages 124–125.

In the meantime Stalin continued his scheming. Needing a government acceptable to the Western powers, he invited the former premier of the government-in-exile, Stanisław Mikołajczyk, from London to Moscow for talks. Minor concessions on Poland's eastern border persuaded Mikołajczyk to accept the vice-premiership in the Provisional Government of National Unity (TRJN) while a communist, Edward Osóbka-Morawski, became its head. In July 1945 the Western powers duly accepted the TRJN as Poland's lawful government.

Over the next two years all power was gradually transferred to the communists. The origins of the Polish communist party can be traced to the Soviet-sponsored Polish Workers' Party (PPR) which held its first congress in December 1945. PPR led a block of socialist and social-democratic parties, the most important of which was Osóbka-Morawski's Polish Socialist Party (PPS). The main opposition group representing democracy was Mikołajczyk's Polish Peasant Party (PSL).

The PPR managed to have elections to the Seym postponed. Instead on 30 April 1946, they arranged a farcical "People's Referendum", in which citizens were asked to vote on issues that had already been decided. Elections were finally held in January 1947, after a

The last conference of the Big Three (USA, Great Britain and the USSR) was held at Potsdam between 17 July and 2 August 1945. Poland's western border with Germany was agreed and Poland was placed firmly in the Soviet sphere.

THE PEOPLE'S REFERENDUM

The 1946 referendum was an attempt to pretend that democracy was still alive in post-war Poland. There were just three questions, to which citizens were expected to vote "3 times YES":

1. Do you approve of the abolition of the Senate?

2. Are you in favour of the affirmation of socio-economic reform?

3. Do you want the western border of Poland affirmed along the Oder and Neisse rivers?

In many regions 80 percent of voters said "no" to question 1, but the communists simply falsified the results.

THE POLISH PEOPLE'S REPUBLIC (PRL) AFTER WORLD WAR II

As a result of the Potsdam Conference Danzig (Gdańsk) and most of East Prussia became Polish. The border with Germany ran south from Stettin (Szczecin) along the Oder (Odra) and Western Neisse (Nysa Łużycka) rivers. The eastern frontier, agreed in Moscow on 16 August 1945, roughly followed the so-called Curzon Line. In effect Poland was shifted westwards by about 200 km. The Polish populations of cities like Wilno and Lwów were relocated, largely in the former German territories. The border with Czechoslovakia was agreed only on 16 June 1958: Zaolzie was given to the Czechs, while Poland gained parts of Spisz, Orawa, Silesian Opole and Kotlina Kłodzka. In January 1946 Poland covered 312,677km^2, and was inhabited by 24 million people.

concerted campaign had weakened the democratic opposition. The elections proceeded in typical Soviet style: a million voters were "disqualified", nearly half the PSL candidates were detained, disqualified or even murdered. The PSL leader Stanisław Mikołajczyk was later accused of espionage and escaped abroad in fear for his life.

And so the communists took power, with Józef Cyrankiewicz as Premier and Bolesław Bierut as President. They quickly began consolidating their position: on 15 December 1948 the PPS and PPR joined forces to create the Polish United Workers' Party (PZPR) – the Polish communist party in all but name. Bierut became its First Secretary and the most powerful man in Poland. The PSL ceased to exist; its surviving members helped create the United Peasant Party (ZSL) – an opposition party independent of the PZPR only in theory.

Stalinist socialism took an ever firmer grip on Poland. Its crowning moment was the passing on 22 July 1952 of a new constitution, which renamed Poland as the Polish People's Republic (PRL). The new constitution had all the outward appearance of a democratic charter but the communists simply ignored it. New legislation was passed in the Seym without serious discussion and unanimously. In reality the Party pulled all the strings of power, assisted by cronies in the dreaded security bureau the *Urząd Bezpieczeństwa* (UB). The workers were often reminded of the vital role they played in political life, but in practice they had no say whatsoever in the running of the country. Censorship grew stricter, and thousands were detained as political prisoners for acts as trivial as grumbling at work.

The standard of living continued to be low. Much of the national budget was spent on the armed forces, and on so-called international assistance to "fraternal people's democracies" such as Angola and Cuba. Millions of dollars worth of coal was shipped free to the Soviet Union, and vast sums went to pay for the upkeep of the Soviet army of occupation in Poland.

After Stalin's death in 1953 communist rule became less despotic and a period known as the "thaw" began. By early 1956 demands for economic reform and the release of political prisoners were being voiced. On 28 June 1956 a strike erupted at the Stalin (former Cegielski) Works in Poznań after staff were cheated of part of their wages. Joined by discontented workers from other factories, the strikers marched on the city centre and seized police stations and government offices. Police and regular army units opened fire, killing 75 and injuring hundreds more. The government insisted the riots had been caused by "foreign agents", but soon admitted that some of the worker's grievances had been justified.

The Poznań riots fuelled divisions in the already weakened Party. The reform-minded liberal Władysław Gomułka offered solutions, and at the Eighth Congress of the Central Committee in October, he was elected as the Party's new leader, without approval from Moscow. The Soviet leader Nikita Krushchev was furious and began massing troops on Poland's borders. He then flew to Warsaw to demand an explanation. After tense

THE PEOPLE'S CONSTITUTION

"Article 1

1. The Polish People's Republic is a people's democracy.

2. In the Polish People's Republic authority resides in the working people of the cities and villages."

The 1952 Constitution stated that all power was in the hands of Poland's workers, who ruled by way of representatives elected to the Sejm. The communists rigged the elections and exploited the Constitution's vague wording to rule as they pleased.

BOLESŁAW BIERUT (1892–1956)

President of Poland (1947––52) and First Secretary of the PZPR (1948–56). A communist activist in the 1930s, he became an agent in the Soviet NKVD after the outbreak of war, and was sent to Warsaw as the leader of the National Home Council (KRN) to seize power for the communists. A firm supporter of Stalin, he was personally responsible for many of the repressive measures introduced in Poland at the height of the Stalinist era.

discussions Gomułka convinced him of his unwavering commitment to communism, and the Soviet tanks stood down. Gomułka proceeded with his reforms: Cardinal Stefan Wyszyński and other priests imprisoned in the early 1950s were released, religious studies were again permitted in schools, and censorship was relaxed. The excesses of Stalinism were curbed, and a new era of small-scale economic activity began.

But Gomułka had no real intention of reforming Poland along Western lines. By the mid-1960s he was losing popularity as it became clear that his economic policies were not working. A hard-line group formed around the interior minister, General Mieczysław Moczar, and gained influence. Moczar advocated a return to Stalinist centralized planning. He saw his chance to oust "softer" elements of the Party soon after the Six Day Arab–Israeli War of 1967 when it became apparent that there was widespread sympathy for the Israelis, whereas Soviet policy required support for the Arabs. A witchhunt followed, with the Jews becoming scapegoats for the government's failures.

Moczar again claimed a Jewish conspiracy was in progress in March 1968. A protest at Warsaw University had been sparked off by the banning of Mickiewicz's anti-Russian play *Dziady* (Forefather's Eve). Moczar provoked violence by ordering the police to disperse the "Zionist-inspired" demonstrators in a heavy-handed manner. Further demonstrations in colleges around the country were violently broken up to give the impression of a breakdown of law and order in the country. The Jews were victimized and more than 13,000 were ordered to leave the country. Yet Moczar failed to obtain power. Meanwhile Gomułka lost his remaining support among the people, especially after he sent Polish troops to help

crush the 1968 Prague Rising in Czechoslovakia.

The Party seemed to be incapable of tackling the economic crisis. In an act of gross mistiming the price of basic foodstuffs was increased by 30 percent just two weeks before Christmas 1970. To Polish workers, whose wages were already inadequate, this assault on their seasonal festivities was intolerable. Public demonstrations in the Baltic Ports were followed by a strike in the Lenin Shipyard in Gdańsk. The army and police were sent in with tanks, and fatalities numbered in the hundreds.

On 20 December 1970 Gomułka, who had suffered a stroke, was replaced as First Secretary by Edward Gierek. A temporary calm over Christmas was followed by a new wave of strikes in January. The strikers' demands now included free trade unions and a free press. Peace was restored only after Gierek had gone personally to the Gdańsk shipyard by taxi, and lowered the price rises.

The first five years of Gierek's rule brought rapid

WŁADYSŁAW GOMUŁKA (1905–1982)

First Secretary (1956–70). Despite his reputation as a liberal, Gomułka had no intention of reforming Poland along Western lines. "Comrade Wiesław", as he was known, had been arrested before World War II for conspiratorial activity and was a firm believer in communist ideals, but hated Stalin's brutal methods. Between 1951 and 1954 he was jailed himself, before his election as Party chief in the "Polish October" of 1956.

EDWARD GIEREK (1913-2001)

First Secretary (1970–80). The first Party leader not to have been "educated" in the USSR, his appointment brought many changes for the better, and improved Poland's contacts with the West. However, his ill-managed programme of industrial renewal and huge loans from Western banks soon took the country to the brink of economic ruin.

THE POZNAŃ RIOTS

On the morning of 28 June 1956 Poznań factory workers occupied the town council offices and the communist party's regional headquarters, and then seized the local jail. However, when they turned on the regional office of the security service (UB) they were fired on. In all about 75 people were killed in the 1956 riots.

POLAND REBORN

SOLIDARITY REMEMBERED

On 16 December 1970 government troops fired on protestors at the Lenin Shipyard in Gdańsk, killing 45 people. One of the concessions won in the 1980 talks was the right to erect a memorial in honour of the victims of the 1970 strike. The monument was also dedicated to those killed in the strikes of 1956 and 1976.

GDAŃSK SHIPYARD

The site of anti-government strikes in 1970 and 1980, the former Lenin Shipyard was the first home of the "Solidarity" trade union movement, and many would say, the true birthplace of democracy in modern Poland.

amount, provoking strikes in Radom, Płock and – most famously – at the Ursus tractor factory near Warsaw, where the main Moscow–Warsaw–Berlin rail route was blocked. Again the militia was called in. Sensing that popular opinion ran deep, the government withdrew the price rises. Key activists were later singled out by the security service. In their defence came the Workers' Defence Committee (KOR), formed in September 1976 by a group of writers and dissidents. It was the start of organized opposition to the communists.

The 1980 Party Congress failed to tackle the continuing economic crisis. In July another wave of strikes hit Silesia, Wielkopolska and the Baltic ports. Before long most factories in the Gdańsk–Gdynia–Sopot conurbation were on strike, leading to formation of the Inter-factory Strike Committee (MKS) in the Gdańsk shipyard under the leadership of Lech Wałęsa. On 31 August, after tense discussions, government representatives agreed to the famous "21 Demands" presented by the strikers. These included the creation of independent trade unions, the release of political prisoners, and the introduction of realistic reforms to take the country out of its economic crisis. The 21 Demands became some-

thing of a manifesto for independence movements throughout Eastern Europe.

In November membership of the independent trade union Solidarity (*Solidarność*) was made legal. The government failed, however, to keep its other promises, and by late 1981 food shortages provoked further demonstrations and strikes. Solidarity's first national congress was held at Gdańsk in September and October. Confident that the nation was firmly behind it, Solidarity demanded far-reaching economic reforms and the democratization of public institutions. The communists at last seemed to be crumbling under the pressure of true "people power".

The growing public euphoria came to an abrupt end on 13 December 1981. With the USSR threatening armed intervention, General Wojciech Jaruzelski (Minister of Defence, Premier, and from 18 October 1981 also First Secretary of the Party) introduced martial law. Thousands of activists were interned, including the Solidarity leadership. Despite intensive searches and the shooting of nine striking miners at the Wujek colliery, underground activity and publishing continued. On 8 October 1982 the Seym passed a resolution on trade unions which made Solidarity illegal. Martial law was eventually suspended at the end of December 1982, but not fully withdrawn until 22 July 1983, and the communists remained firmly in control.

To many whose hopes had been raised in the heady days of 1981, Poland had lost its way. The frustration and lack of opportunities at home caused many of the brightest and more energetic persons to emigrate; others sought solace in drink. The Catholic Church stood as a pillar in these hard times, and increasingly took on an anti-communist stance. The murder of a priest, Jerzy Popiełuszko, by members of the security services on 19 October 1984

MARTIAL LAW

In a TV broadcast on Sunday 13 December 1981, General Wojciech Jaruzelski announced a state of emergency in Poland. Tanks appeared on the streets, and a curfew was imposed from 10pm to 6am. About 10,000 political activists were arrested.

was seen by many as the final straw. A new sense of purpose began to stir; even the release of political prisoners in 1986 did little to defuse the situation.

Between April and August 1988 yet another wave of strikes paralysed the country. Reluctantly the Party agreed to consider fundamental changes in the structure of government. In truth, the climb-down owed much to the rise to power in Moscow of Mikhail Gorbachev.

The final breakthrough came with the Round Table talks of 6 February – 5 April 1989. Solidarity was re-legalized, freedom of the press was guaranteed, and "semi-free elections" were promised. The elections went ahead in June. All 100 seats in the newly re-established Senate were won by the Solidarity camp; in the lower house, the Seym, Solidarity received its maximum permitted allowance of 35 percent of the seats. In July the combined chambers chose General Jaruzelski as President of Poland by a majority of just one vote. In August he asked Solidarity activist and journalist Tadeusz Mazowiecki to form the first non-communist government since the war. One of its first acts, at the end of 1989, was to restore the old name of the country – the Polish Republic. The first presidential elections took place on 22 December 1990, and, to widespread euphoria, were won by Lech Wałęsa.

The political changes in Poland sparked off similar reforms in the other states of eastern Europe: Czechoslovakia, East Germany, Hungary, Romania and Bulgaria. They also contributed to the collapse of the USSR.

The Polish communist party, the PZPR, disbanded itself at the beginning of 1990, although many members went on to form a new party – Social Democracy of the Polish Republic (SDRP). In the 1995 election, in res-ponse to the painful transition to a free market economy, the "post-communist" candidate Aleksander Kwaśniewski ousted Wałęsa to become President for two terms of office. On 23 December 2005 Lech Kaczyński was sworn in as the third President of democratic Poland.

LECH WAŁĘSA (BORN 1943)

Co-founder of "Solidarity" and President of Poland (1990–95). An electrician by trade, he worked in the Gdańsk shipyard where, in 1970, he became a member of the strike committee. From August 1980 he became internationally famous as head of the new Inter-factory Strike Committee. In 1989 he led the opposition during the Round Table talks, and in 1990 was elected President of Poland.

Born as a trade union during the Gdańsk Shipyard strike of 1980, Solidarity soon had about ten million members and was the *de facto* opposition party to the communist government by 1981. Banned under Martial Law, Solidarity took the helm again in 1986 and, with the worsening economic situation, forced the government to negotiate.

At the "Round Table" talks of February to April 1989 (*left*), the "Solidarity-Opposition" camp sat down with the Government Coalition and hammered out the comprises needed to bring democracy to Poland.

THE POLISH POPE

Cardinal Karol Wojtyła became Pope John Paul II on 16 October 1978. His visits to Poland in 1979 and 1983 created huge gatherings and focused world-wide attention on Poland's plight. During the darkest years of the 1980s he was a symbol that Poland would eventually overcome communism. John Paul II died on 2 April 2005.

CARDINAL STEFAN WYSZYŃSKI (1901–1981)

A chaplain in the Home Army in World War II, he stood up repeatedly in defence of human and civil rights during four decades of communist rule, and was held in custody from 1953 to 1956. As Primate of the Catholic Church in Poland he was the moral leader of Polish society in the 1970s, and his funeral in 1981 became a huge demonstration of patriotism.

ECONOMY AND CULTURE IN THE 20TH CENTURY

To Poles the 20th century has been a hard test of character. First came the challenges of rebuilding the nation after the destruction of not one, but two world wars. More recently there has been the problem of creating a free market economy after decades of neglect under the communists.

Reborn in 1918, Poland inherited from the Partitioning Powers a country in economic ruin. Plundered of machines and factory tools, with a poor, illiterate and overpopulated rural scene, the country faced daunting challenges. Wielkopolska was the only region to have adopted modern agricultural practices; the Russian areas were agriculturally backward but had textile as well as mining and smelting industries; Galicia meanwhile was retarded in both farming and industry.

The government rightly saw education as the reborn nation's first priority. Illiteracy was common and teachers were in short supply. In the first months after independence, the groundwork for free primary education for all was laid in place. In their turn the middle and higher education systems were expanded, and public libraries were opened. Scientific bodies were set up, including the highly regarded Polish Academy of Learning (*Polska Akademia Umiejętności*).

By the end of 1924 the wartime damage to the ra[] network had been repaired and 168km of new "iron roads" had been laid to connect up the separate rail networks c the Partitioning Powers. The first Polish-built stea[] engines and wagons also soon appeared.

Among the other successes of the two interwar decade was the development of new branches of industry – chem[] cals, weapons, and motor vehicles. In 1922, thanks to th[] efforts of vice-premier Eugeniusz Kwiatkowski, work bega[] on the construction of Poland's "window on the world" the new port of Gdynia. It allowed free trade abroad, whic[] until then had been hindered by the German authorities [

THE PORT OF GDYNIA

The building from new of a Baltic port was Poland's largest civil project of the interwar years. The person responsible was the engineer and chemist Eugeniusz Kwiatkowski (1888–1974), vice-premier and minister of finance. He also played a part in the creation of Poland's merchant fleet.

MONETARY REFORM

In 1919 Russian roubles, Austrian koronas, German marks and later Polish marks circulated in Poland. They were replaced in April 1924 by a new single currency – the *złoty*, which was divided into 100 *groszy*. The main architect of the monetary reform was Władysław Grabski, premier (1923–25), and minister of finance.

the Free City of Danzig (Gdańsk). A further boost to trade was created by the annual international trade fairs organized in Poznań from 1925. Perhaps the largest project of the late 1930s was the creation of the Central Industrial District (COP), which employed over 100,000 workers in the strategically important Kielce–Lublin–Kraków–Lwów region in the south of the country.

Insurmountable problems came with the trade war with Germany (1925–31), and the worldwide Great Depression which struck after the Wall Street Crash of 1929. Both retarded the growth of the Polish economy into the 1930s. Despite great advances, the 20-year inter-war period proved to be too short to bring Poland's industry and communications infrastructure up to Western standards. Most of Poland remained backward and rural, hampered by a lack of investment. High unemployment further depressed living standards in urban areas.

The massive devastation of World War II meant that much of the hard work of the interwar years had to be repeated. Proportionately Poland suffered the most serious destruction of all the countries involved in the war,

and needed rebuilding on an even greater scale than after World War I. The integration of East Prussia and the western territories received as part of the German war reparations were further problems.

Despite the presence of Soviet troops, a genuine enthusiasm among the population meant that the rubble was cleared and destroyed buildings were rapidly replaced. The city of Warsaw, more than 80 percent of which had been flattened by Hitler's demolition squads, soon began to rise again, phoenix-like, out of the ashes.

Unfortunately, by 1947 things began to turn for the worse as Stalin's inhuman methods were introduced. In accordance with the new "fraternal friendship" with the USSR, a programme of nationalization took place from 1946. Firms were placed under state control. Private shops and warehouses disappeared as the state took charge of trade. Poland became a "planned economy" – in which the evils of profit and private ownership were to be rigorously avoided. Experienced professionals such as Eugeniusz Kwiatkowski were sacked, and new "specialists" were appointed to follow blindly the Soviet model.

THE NATIONAL EXHIBITION (PEWUKA)

Opened on 16 May 1929 in Poznań by President Mościcki, the Universal National Exhibition (Pewuka) was intended to show the world how much Poland had achieved in the first decade of independence. Organized on the site of the International Poznań Trade Fair (*photo below*), the event was a great success, attracting about 4 million visitors.

THE SEYM

Built between 1925 and 1928 on Wiejska street in Warsaw, the Seym building has columns and a frieze inspired by the architecture of the world's oldest democracy – ancient Greece. The building is still in use today, with the hall under the dome seating the 460 members of the Seym. The 100-member Senate holds sessions in a separate chamber.

The new communist authorities, despite earlier promises, now attempted to overturn the 1944 agricultural reforms which had, after centuries, finally given the peasants their own land. Peasant small-holdings were forcibly combined into communal farms. Larger collective farms were created on the Soviet model, especially in the former German territories; the Russian term for such farms, *Kolkhoz*, was carefully avoided and instead they were termed State Agricultural Units (*Państwowe Gospodarstwa Rolne* – PGR). However, the collectivization programme failed abysmally to increase output, and was abandoned in the 1950s.

In the early 1950s Poland's heavy industries received the same Soviet treatment, with mixed success. Work began on several gigantic projects, the largest of which was the steel town of Nowa Huta near Kraków. Coal mining was expanded in Silesia, and a whole shipbuilding industry developed in the Baltic ports. Little attention was paid, however, to providing reasonable living conditions for workers, nor to the dreadful pollution such industries produced. The building of such dinosaurs continued despite Stalin's death in 1953.

Władysław Gomułka's rise to power in 1956 brought a "thaw" in Stalinism and some of the more obvious excesses were eliminated. Gomułka's ideas of small-scale economics and self-reliance were widely adopted, and Poland became the only country behind the Iron Curtain where the land area worked by private farmers exceeded that managed by the state.

NOWA HUTA

The construction of a new steel town of 100,000 inhabitants began near Kraków in 1949 as a typical example of communist architecture and social engineering. The location was selected not because of the availability of raw materials (coal has to come 90km by rail from Silesia), but rather because Kraków was seen as dangerously "intellectual" and in need of dilution by ordinary workers. The terrible pollution damage to Kraków's historic monuments was not considered.

SOCIALIST REALISM

The new art of communism was intended to have a moral message. Its heroes were the ordinary workers and peasants, who were building a "new future" for the communal good. The new style, known as Socialist Realism, borrowed greatly from Soviet art, and reached its peak in the 1950s. A good example is Aleksander Kobzdej's painting *Podaj cegłę* (Pass me a brick) dedicated to the bricklayers who were building the nation anew.

PALACE OF CULTURE

Built in Warsaw between 1952 and 1955, the gargantuan Palace of Culture and Science was a "fraternal" gift from the Soviet Union.

The appointment in 1970 of First Secretary Edward Gierek brought a new era of grand economics. He convinced Western banks to loan him $24 billion for turning Poland into a "second Japan". The money was intended to modernize the extraction of Poland's raw material reserves, and to build new factories. These, in turn, were to export manufactured goods to repay the loans. But building projects were delayed and the new goods were of poor quality. The oil crisis and world recession in the 1970s also meant that the returns were lower than expected. By the 1980s Poland was exporting everything available to service the loans, leading to shortages in almost all consumer goods. Eventually it was the spiralling mountain of foreign debt – close to $40 billion – and the economic crisis that it caused which brought down the communist system.

With the elections of 4 June 1989 Poland at last turned to an economy based on the free market. In 1991 the International Monetary Fund (IMF) agreed to halve the outstanding national debt providing that Poland followed Western economic practices. An austerity programme led to hyper-inflation and painful unemployment. Paradoxically, it was a medicine much harsher than that thought acceptable under the communists.

A perceptible buzz of optimism can now be felt in the newly refurbished streets of Warsaw. In July 1997 Poland was invited to join NATO, and has realistic hopes of becoming a member of the European Union within the next decade. With the economy in the late-1990s growing at above 5 percent – among the fastest in Europe – Poland looks forward to a bright and prosperous future in the 21st century.

The ups and downs of Polish economics have to a large extent been mirrored in art and culture. Poland's reborn independence inspired works full of optimism.

SOCIALIST DREAM, PRIVATE NIGHTMARE

A typical view in the typical modern Polish city. Poznań's Winogrady housing estate was built from 1968 to cope with post-war housing shortages. It is an example of the inhuman realities behind the the communist dream.

AN ECONOMY IN CRISIS

The socialist dream began to turn sour in the 1970s. Inefficiencies in distribution and the desperate need for hard currency to repay foreign loans meant that first food, and then consumer goods such as shoes and cigarettes disappeared from the shops. It was only possible to buy them with ration cards, and then in limited quantities. This card is for the total monthly allowance of meat for a single citizen – 2.5kg. Even with the ration system, mothers with families to feed still regularly had to wait in line for several hours for a single cut of meat. It was a damning verdict on communism that in an agriculturally rich country like Poland, which produces far more food than it needs, the shelves were empty save for buckwheat and vinegar.

MODERN TIMES

The reforms of the 1990s have seen the rapid modernization of Poland's cities. Luxurious new hotels, marble-faced banks and supermarkets full of goods have sprung up like mushrooms; the streets are lined with colourful advertising hoardings, and bustle with cars from all parts of the world.

There is, however, still a very great task ahead before the 50 years of neglect and poor planning under the communists can be fully remedied.

Many artists followed the latest avant-garde trends, fascinated by the ultra modern (technology, city life and futurism) or by expressionism, with its stress on inner feelings and personal experience. The gloomy, catastrophic works that appeared in the 1930s were portents of the coming war.

World War II produced brilliant poetry – but as so often, this was inseparable from tragedy. The poets Krzysztof Kamil Baczyński and Tadeusz Gajcy both died when barely in their twenties during the 1944 Warsaw Rising. Many writers and painters fled overseas; others suffered the horrors of the Nazi and Soviet concentration camps. Among the survivors who later recounted their experiences were Tadeusz Borowski and Gustaw Herling-Grudziński.

The communist era had an insipid influence on Polish art. In 1949, at the Polish Literary Congress in Szczecin, delegates agreed to adopt the Soviet-approved school of "Socialist Realism". The new style was intended to appeal to ordinary working Poles and to inspire them to work harder for the good of the state. Anything with historical roots was denounced as "bourgeois". Socialist Realism replaced beauty and elegance with the functional and mundane. Its influence was felt most of all in architecture, which as an artform came to an abrupt halt. Forty years of Socialist Realism have resulted in the scarring of Poland's urban and rural landscapes with architectural monstrosities which may take decades to remove.

To their credit, the communist authorities went to great lengths to rebuild the education system. But the teaching profession, so important before the war, lost much of its status. In 1951 the Polish Academy of Sciences (PAN) was created, albeit mostly from a desire to centralize and control. It nevertheless became a world-class scientific institutution.

The second half of the 20th century has seen an enormous change in popular culture in the age of radio, film and television. The communists realized at once the

POLISH NOBEL PRIZE WINNERS FOR LITERATURE

The Nobel Prize for literature was first awarded in 1901. To date the prize has been won by four Poles:

HENRYK SIENKIEWICZ (1846–1916)

The author of Poland's greatest historical novels, including *The Deluge* (Potop) set during Poland's 17th-century wars. He received the Nobel Prize in 1905 for his Biblical epic *Quo vadis*.

WŁADYSŁAW REYMONT (1867–1925)

Author of the hyper-realisitic novels *Promised Land* (Ziemia obiecana) and *Peasants*. The latter won him the 1924 Prize for its portrayal of the natural rhythms of life in a Polish village.

CZESŁAW MIŁOSZ (1911–2004)

Poet, novelist, translator and diplomat, he settled in the USA in 1960. His work vocalizes the psychological scars received in World War II and under the communists. He won the 1980 Prize.

WISŁAWA SZYMBORSKA (BORN 1923)

A poet able to describe everyday events in the most surprising, revelatory manner. Author of nine small volumes including *Calling out to Yeti*, *The People on the Bridge*, and *End and Beginning*, *Moment* and *Colon*. She was awarded the 1996 Prize.

POLISH RADIO AND TELEVISION

Poland's first trial radio-station began transmitting in 1925, and regular services from Warsaw commenced one year later. In 1931 Poland boasted the most powerful radio-transmitter in the world (120kW, at Raszyn near Warsaw), and by 1939, Polish radio had over 1 million regular listeners.

Poland's first public television broadcast took place in Warsaw in December 1951. Regular black-and-white transmissions began in May 1956, colour in 1970.

power of the new mass media, and imposed strict censorship soon after they came to power. In frustration, many of the most creative personalities left Poland, only to have their output subsequently banned in their homeland. By about 1975 an artistic underground had developed in Poland, issuing newspapers and books. It was only through this, and foreign radio broadcasts (notably those of Radio Free Europe) that Poles were able to access the free exchange of ideas in the West.

Nevertheless, a thriving (if cautious) literary and art scene continued in Poland. One of the greatest services of communism was the realization that artistic activities require state support, and this was given generously. In particular the Polish film industry became respected throughout the West.

In 1989 all the artistic barriers were suddenly pulled down, but the "new realities" of the 1990s have brought mixed reactions. Art is once more able to develop unfettered. But many believe Polish culture now has an even harder task ahead if it is to maintain its identity and survive against the flood of material from abroad – mainly via satellite television.

A VERY POLISH DRAMA

Adam Mickiewicz's classic play *Dziady* (Forefather's Eve) caused a nationwide sensation in February 1968, when a performance in Warsaw's National Theatre was closed on the whim of the Soviet ambassador. Protests in universities across Poland were suppressed with violence. The photograph shows a scene from the controversial 1968 performance, directed by Kazimierz Dejmek.

POLISH CINEMA

Poland's first movie was the 1908 travel story: *Antoś's First Trip to Warsaw*. The first post-war movie (*above*) was *Forbidden Songs* (1947), about life in Nazi-occupied Warsaw. The Polish film industry has a high international reputation, with directors of such calibre as Andrzej Wajda and Krzysztof Kieślowski.

CHRONOLOGY

c.738–400 BC Heyday of the Biskupin settlement

c.960 AD Beginning of Mieszko I's reign

966 Mieszko I is baptised; Poland joins the community of Latin Christian countries

972 Battle of Cedynia

1000 German emperor Otto III visits Bolesław Chrobry's court • Poland's first archbishop is established at Gniezno

1025 Bolesław Chrobry is crowned king of Poland

1138 King Bolesław Krzywousty divides the Polish lands among his sons; the 200-year period of fragmentation begins, with Poland broken up into small dukedoms

1226 The Teutonic Knights are invited to Poland by Konrad of Mazovia

1241 Mongols devastate southern Poland, burning towns and fortresses; Polish forces are defeated at the battle of Legnica

1320 Władysław Łokietek is crowned king of a reunited Poland

1370 Death of Kazimierz the Great, last king of the Piast dynasty

1385 Union of Krewo: Poland and Lithuania are joined in "personal union" by the marriage of Queen Jadwiga and Władysław Jagiełło

1410 Battle of Grunwald–Tannenberg

1454–66 Thirteen Years' War between Poland and the Teutonic Knights, ending with the Peace of Toruń (1466)

c.1493 Foundation of the Seym (diet or parliament), made up of the Senate and the Chamber of Deputies

1525 The Prussian Homage: the former Grand Master of the Teutonic Knights, Albrecht von Hohenzollern, swears allegiance to the king of Poland

1569 Union of Lublin: Poland is formally joined with Lithuania to became a "Commonwealth of Two Nations"

1572 Death of Zygmunt II August, last king of the Jagiellonian dynasty

1573 First "Free Election" of the king of Poland by the noblemen • Freedom of religious worship is guaranteed by the Warsaw Convocational Seym

1620–21 Polish–Turkish War: the Polish army is defeated at Cecora (1620), but wins a great victory at Chocim (1621)

1652 First use of the *Liberum Veto* to break up the Seym • Polish army is annihilated by Chmielnicki's Ukrainian rebels at the battle of Batoh

1655–57 The Swedes invade and devastate Poland in the so-called "Deluge"

1683 Relief of Vienna: Turkish forces besieging the Imperial capital are defeated by a Polish–Austrian army under Jan III Sobieski

1772 First Partition of Poland

1773 Founding of the National Education Commission

1788–92 The Great Seym (also called the Four Year Seym)

1791 Passing of Poland's Constitution (on 3rd May) – the first such in Europe and the second in the world after that of America

1793 Second Partition of Poland

1794 The Kościuszko Insurrection

1795 Third Partition of Poland; the country ceases to exist as a sovereign power for the following 123 years

1797 Polish Legions formed in Italy by Jan Henryk Dąbrowski

1807 Napoleon sets up the Duchy of Warsaw

1815 The Vienna Congress creates the "Congress Kingdom" of Poland, under Russian supervision; also formed is the small Kraków Republic and the Grand Duchy of Poznań

1830–31 The November Rising

1848 "Spring of the Peoples": Popular risings in Wielkopolska and Galicia

1863–64 The January Rising

1901 Schoolchildren's strike at Września in Wielkopolska

1905–07 Polish workers play an active part in the First Russian Revolution

1914 World War I begins • Polish legions are formed by Józef Piłsudski in Galicia to fight alongside the Austrians against the Russians

1918 US President Woodrow Wilson declares that a key condition for world peace is an independent Poland • Russia declares the partitioning of Poland void • Germany and Austria surrender • Józef Piłsudski becomes Poland's head-of-state

1918–19 The Poznań (or Wielkopolska) Rising, prompted by the wave of patriotism following the arrival in Poznań of the composer Paderewski

1919 Poland's frontiers with Germany are decided at the Paris Peace Conference

1919–21 The Polish–Soviet War culminates in the "Miracle on the Vistula" (August 1920) • A popular referendum (Plebiscite) in Upper Silesia results in three Silesian Risings

1921 Passing of a new Constitution for the Polish Republic (the so-called March Constitution)

1926 Józef Piłsudski topples the government by a *coup d'etat* • The new regime introduces the *Sanacja* programme to "clean up" the inefficient political system

1935 Passing of the April Constitution, which strengthens the powers of the President

1939 Nazi Germany invades Poland, sparking off World War II • The Soviet Union treacherously seizes eastern Poland • A Polish government-in-exile is formed in the West with General Władysław Sikorski at its head • Polish armed forces reassemble in France and Syria

1940 Polish troops fight in the battle for Norway (at Narvik), and in defence of France; with the fall of France, they evacuate to Great Britain • Polish airmen win fame in the Battle of Britain • The Nazis build their largest concentration camp at Oświęcim (Auschwitz)

1941
Nazi Germany launches a surprise attack on the USSR • A Polish–Soviet accord signed in London allows General Władysław Anders to begin forming a Polish Army in the USSR • Independent Carpathian Rifle Brigade takes part in the defence of Tobruk in North Africa

1942–43
Anders' Army is evacuated from the USSR to Iran • The Soviets break off relations with the Polish government in London • 1st "Kościuszko" Infantry Division is the first of many Polish formations raised in the USSR under communist supervision

1943–44
The National Home Council (KRN) and the Lublin Committee (PKWN) are formed as Soviet puppet organizations to take control of liberated Poland

1944
The Warsaw Rising (1 Aug –2 October) fails due to lack of support from Stalin • Polish formations take part in the liberation of Italy, France, Belgium and Holland

1945
The war in Europe ends (8 May) soon after the fall of Berlin • The Provisional Government of National Unity (TRJN) is formed • Poland's western border on the Oder and Neisse rivers is decided at the Potsdam Conference

1946
The People's Referendum seeks to legitimize communist rule in Poland

1952
Passing of the Constitution of the Polish People's Republic

1956
Strikes and mass demonstrations in Poznań leave 75 dead • The "thaw" in Stalinism begins: Gomułka introduces the first liberal reforms

1968
A performance of Mickiewicz's play *Dziady* is banned, provoking student demonstrations which are broken up with excessive violence

1970
Strikes in the Baltic ports

1976
Strikes at Radom, Ursus and Płock

1978
Cardinal Karol Wojtyła becomes Pope as John Paul II

1980
Countrywide strikes led by the independent trade union *Solidarność*

1981
General Jaruzelski declares martial law

1989
"Round Table" talks held in Warsaw • *Solidarność* wins a resounding victory in the first post-war elections to the Seym and Senate

1990
• First free presidential election since the war, Lech Wałęsa wins

1999
• Poland becomes NATO member

2004
• Poland joins UE

2005
• Pope John Paul II dies after a 27-year-long pontificate

2007
• Poland in Schengen zone – Europe without borders

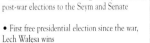

GLOSSARY OF HISTORICAL TERMS

Arians . . . . A Protestant religious sect active in Poland during the 16th and 17th centuries. They derived from the Hussites of Bohemia, and were known by many names including the Polish Brethren, Socinians and Anti-Trinitarians. The most famous of their schools, the Raków Academy, was renowned for its novel teaching methods. The Arians valued honesty, and carried wooden swords to show they did not believe in the shedding of blood. They were expelled from Poland in 1658.

Castellan . . . . (Pol. *kasztelan*) Originally the administrator of a *gród* (fortified town). It later became an honorary rank, which gave a seat in the Senate.

Commonwealth . . . . Approximate English translation of *Rzeczpospolita* (from Latin *res publica,* literally "thing of the people"), referring to the federal state of Poland and Lithuania from 1569 to 1795.

Confederation . . . . (Pol. *Konfederacja*). A revolt, directed usually at the king or his representatives.

Congress Kingdom . . . . (Pol. *Kongresówka*).The Polish state created by the Congress of Vienna in 1815; the tsar of Russia was its hereditary king. After the November Rising of 1831 it kept its name, but became an administrative district of the Russian empire. In 1864 it was renamed the "Vistula Land".

Cossacks. Warlike people of the Russian Steppes; in Polish usage it refers specifically to the Ruthenian peasant-soldiers of the Ukraine who, in the 17th century, attempted to break away from Polish rule and to create their own state.

Crown . . . . (Pol. *Korona*) the Kingdom of Poland – the Polish heartland of the Polish–Lithuanian Commonwealth, as distinct from the Grand Duchy of Lithuania.

Curzon Line. . . . . Polish-Russian frontier proposed in December 1919 after the Versailles Conference and named after British foreign secretary Lord Curzon (1859–1925). It ran along the eastward edge of ethnically Polish land. In 1945 Poland's eastern border was chosen to follow, more or less, the Curzon Line.

Estate. . . . . A section of society with its own laws and privileges. In medieval times the upper estates – the *nobility* and *clergy* – were expected to run the country and to provide for spiritual needs, while the lower estates – the *commons* – provided for the worldly needs of the upper estates. The word is similar but not identical in meaning to "class".

Excommunication . . . . Formal expulsion of an offender from the Roman Catholic Church. In the age when the Church held great power as well as spiritual influence, excommunication was a severe and greatly feared punishment.

Feudal Levy. . . . . (Pol. *Pospolite ruszenie*, French *Levée-en-Masse*). Body of noblemen who owed military service to the state in return for their privileges. Although largely replaced by paid troops by the 1460s, the cumbersome institution was not abolished. In 1794 the term was applied to peasants as well as nobles, and attempts were made to raise it again in the risings of 1806 and 1831.

Folwark . . . . A farm estate, usually linked to a nobleman's manor. In the 16th-century they became popular especially in Ukraine, where Polish noblemen grew huge amounts of corn for export. These estates were largely responsible for the growth of serfdom and so precipitated the Ukrainian rebellions of the 17th century.

Gród (Plural Grody). . . . . A fortified town or stronghold, which from about the 10th century became a base for frontier defence and an administrative centre.

Grosze . . . . (From German *Groschen*) A monetary unit, equal to 1/100 (previously 1/32) of a Polish złoty. It derived from the medieval Latin *denarius grossus* (thick penny), a silver coin of small denomination.

Herb. . . . . Polish clan-badge, roughly equivalent to a coat-of-arms. Polish heraldry is quite different from that of other European countries, and many noble families share the same badge without being related.

Hetman . . . . Supreme commander of the army (15th–18th centuries). The *Hetman Wielki* (Grand Hetman) was overall commander, while the *Hetman Polny* (Field Hetman) was second-in-command, responsible for the standing army and defence against Tatar raids. Between 1569 and 1795 there were separate Hetmans for Poland and Lithuania. An additional "Hetman of the Zaporozhian Army" commanded the Ukrainian Cossack auxiliary forces.

Homage. (Pol. *Hołd*). Public acknowledgement of allegiance to a king or lord. In the medieval ceremony the vassal "paying homage" knelt before his lord and swore to be faithful to him.

Interregnum. . . . . Literally "between reigns" – the interval between the end of a monarch's rule and the accession of a successor. Authority passed temporarily to the *Prymas*, who became *interrex* or "between-king".

Liberum Veto . . . . The right of any individual deputy to stop proceedings of the Seym by his single dissenting vote. First invoked in 1652, it was to have a catastrophic effect on the ability of the Seym to conduct reform, and has been blamed for the "Polish anarchy" of the 18th century. However, it was not invoked as often as generally believed, and had been abandoned by 1764. As the linchpin of the "Golden Freedom" of the nobles, it was not abolished until 1791.

Livonia . . . . (Polish *Inflanty*, German *Livland*) Former region on the eastern Baltic coast, comprising most of modern Latvia and Estonia. Conquered in the early 13th century by German knights, it became a semi-independent province of the Teutonic Order. In the 16th, 17th and 18th centuries it was disputed by Sweden, Denmark, Russia and Poland.

Łan . . . . A measure of land area. It originally represented the land "held in loan" by a single farmer and his household, and was the fundamental unit of peasant labour dues and noble land taxes. It later became a more precise unit of area, varying between 17 and 26 hectares (40–60 acres).

Magnat . . . . Magnate or baron; member of a small group of families whose huge wealth and control of high state offices set them apart from the ordinary *szlachta* or nobles.

Małopolska . . . . Little Poland (or Lesser Poland) Province in south-eastern Poland, centred on Kraków. It was the smaller part of the lands of the Polanian dukes, and was based on the former territories of the Slavic Vislani tribe.

March . . . . (Pol. *marchia*, from German *Mark*) Border district of the German empire established between 9th and 13th centuries, usually out of land captured from the Slavs.

Margrave . . . . (Pol. *margrabia*, from German *Markgraf*, literally "count of the March") German title for the ruler of a border province or *march*. His legal powers, especially in matters of war, were greater than those of an ordinary count. By the 16th century the title was no longer reserved for border lords.

Old Prussians . . . . (Pol. *Prusy*) A now-extinct non-Slavic people. Also known as the *Pruzzi* or *Bruzzi*, they were related to the Lithuanians and other Baltic peoples. They inhabited the region of northern Poland (roughly Warmia and Mazuria) until virtually exterminated by the Knights of the Teutonic Order. The latinized name *Prussia* remained as a geographical term, and when the German Order was secularized in the 16th century, its lands became the Duchy of Prussia.

Pańszczyzna . . . . Labour dues – the obligation of a peasant to work for his lord for a number of days per week.

Piast . . . . The first ruling dynasty of Poland, so called after a legendary figure, Piast the common farmer. The term was first used by historians in the 17th century; it was also applied to native Polish candidates in the royal elections of the 17th and 18th centuries.

Plebiscite . . . . Referendum or vote of the citizens of a country or region to decide an important issue. Plebiscites were employed after World War I to determine whether Upper Silesia and parts of East Prussia/Warmia and Mazuria should belong to Poland or to Germany.

Posnania . . . . Popular name for the Duchy of Posen (Poznań), 1815–1848, then part of the Kingdom of Prussia.

Prymas . . . . The Primate or head of the Catholic Church in Poland, usually the senior archbishop. He held political as well as religious powers and, in the period of elected kings, was head of state in the event of an *interregnum*.

Ruthenia . . . . (Pol. *Ruś*) Historical term for the region immediately to the east of modern Poland, inhabited by "Lesser Russians" as opposed to the "Great Russians" of Moscow. It corresponds to the modern states of Byelorussia, Lithuania and Ukraine.

Senate . . . . (Pol. *Senat*) The higher chamber of the Seym.

Seym . . . . (Pol. *Sejm*, originally spelt *Seym*) Diet or parliament. A legislative body of noblemen, which from about 1500 was Poland's main executive instrument of state.

Seymik . . . . Dietine, or local assembly. A gathering of noblemen in a region or province of the *Commonwealth*, which from the 16th century began to have considerable local powers. Each seymik elected deputies to the *Seym*.

Socialism . . . . In late-20th century East European usage, often a euphemism for what Westerners call "communism".

Starosta . . . . (Literally "elder") A high officer appointed by the king, holding a castle and land, which he was required to administer. He also had legal, civil and military powers and the right to collect taxes.

Szlachta . . . . Pol. *Nobleman*, or the noble *estate* in general. From 1374 all nobles had the same rights and regarded themselves as equals. By the late 17th century they numbered 10 percent of the population.

Tsar . . . . The ruler or emperor of Russia, a term derived from the Roman imperial title "Caesar".

Wielkopolska . . . . "Greater Poland" – the heart of the ancient kingdom of Poland, based around Poznań and Gniezno.

Wojewoda . . . . (Often translated into English as *palatine* or *voivode*) Governor of a province; in modern usage – an official in charge of an administrative district (*województwo*) roughly equivalent to an English county.

Acknowledgements

The publishers Publicat Joint-stock Comp.
would graciously like to thank:
Biblioteka Raczyńskich, Poznań (especially Jakub Skutecki)
Biblioteka Uniwersytecka, Poznań
Tadeusz Jeziorowski – director of the Muzeum Wojskowe, Poznań
Zdzisław Moliński – curator of the Castle in Rydzyna
Filmoteka Narodowa
Instytut Sztuki, Warsaw (and Ms. Myszkowska)
Muzeum Dzieci Wrzesińskich, Września
Muzeum Kolejnictwa, Warsaw
Muzeum Lotnictwa, Kraków
Towarzystwo Numizmatyczne, Poznań
Anna Winiecka
And everyone who assisted in the creation of this book.